THE ANCIENT GREEKS

NEW YORK

OXFORD UNIVERSITY PRESS

LONDON 1971 TORONTO

THE
ANCIENT
GREEKS

CHESTER G. STARR

PROFESSOR OF ANCIENT HISTORY

UNIVERSITY OF MICHIGAN

Sixth printing, 1978
Copyright © 1971 by Oxford University Press, Inc.
Library of Congress Catalogue Card Number: 78-124613
Printed in the United States of America

CONTENTS

PART II · The Expansion of Greek Civilization

PART III · Sources on Athenian Democracy and Imperialism

Special Topics

Sources of Quotations   213

Further Reading   215

Glossary   219

PART I

The Rise of Greek Civilization

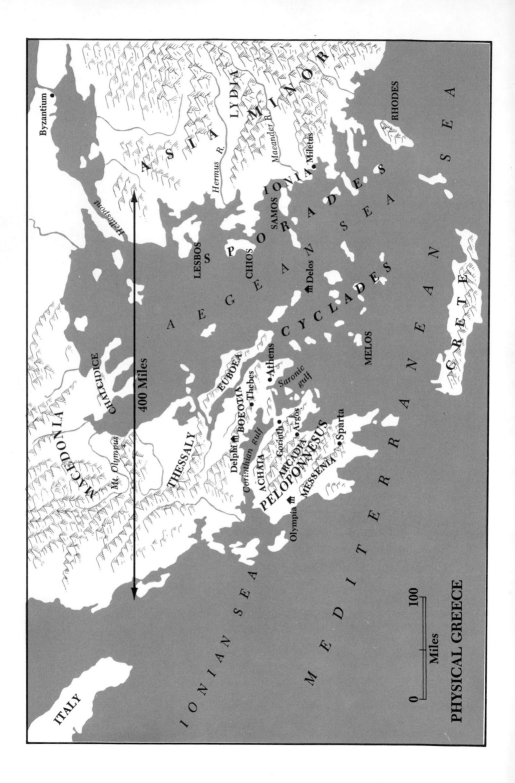

PHYSICAL GREECE

Looking out over the Aegean islands

Photo by Harissiadis—Athens

Why learn about the ancient Greeks? That is the obvious question for anyone living today and dreaming about tomorrow, for the Greeks have been dead a long time.

One answer is clear: these are the people who began our civiliza- ˙ tion. Much of the world around us at this moment was created only yesterday, or the day before yesterday; and we all expect new marvels tomorrow. Machines or institutions, however, are the fruit of ideas, beliefs, and skills which do not change rapidly. Our way of thought, called Western civilization, is based on political, artistic, and intellectual principles which can be traced from the modern Western world to medieval Europe, from medieval Europe to ancient Rome, and from Rome to Greece.

Farther back we cannot go, for the Greeks "began" it. True, they inherited from other peoples many of their techniques, such as farming, metal working, and writing; but whatever they inherited was altered and transformed into something virtually new. The alphabet is Phoenician in origin, for example; the Greeks made some symbols stand for vowels (which the Phoenicians did not write) and turned the alphabet into a supple tool with which they could set down all types of thought precisely and clearly.

The word "political" is Greek; from Greek political theory we derive the belief that a citizen has rights as well as duties within his state. The word "esthetic" is Greek; and artists throughout the centuries have drawn inspiration from Greek art. The "geometry" we may have studied in "school" is that set down by Euclid, a Greek. "Philosophy" and "logic," "poetry" and "tragedy," "machine" and "physics" are all words invented by the Greeks; but more than being just words each stands for an important concept or way of analyzing our world.

This is certainly significant. From the Greeks came so many of our mental skills and techniques that one could almost say they discovered the mind. But if we stress only the importance of the Greeks, we shall forget a second reason for looking at them—the fact that they were among the most fascinating peoples ever to live.

One of the main values of history is that it throws light on the nature of man, his strengths and his weaknesses. From this point of view the story of the Greeks is absorbing. They had a fresh, youthful enthusiasm and felt nothing was impossible; at the same time they gazed at life coolly and frankly and never glossed over its ills. One of their poets said of an old man that "to children he is hateful, to women contemptible, so grievous has the divine spirit made Age." Some Greeks were great political or intellectual heroes; others were bloodthirsty and traitorous. A Greek tragedy like *Oedipus the King* or *Agamemnon* may appear at first reading to be a lesson in reason and balanced serenity; but below the surface lurk as much murder, adultery, and ruthless passion as in any modern movie. The Greeks are one of the rare peoples in history who were never dull.

CHAPTER 1

The Background of Greek History

Geography and Climate. If we are to understand the progress and achievements of the amazing Greeks, we must place them against their background. In many important respects their background differed from ours. To mention only those aspects which will be considered here, the landscape and climate of Greece were markedly unlike those of continental Europe and those of North America; the ways of making a living were far simpler; and man's daily existence was felt to be controlled in every respect by religious forces.

First, the landscape. Greek history was not simply an expression of the geographic framework, but the influences of its local conditions and its position in the Mediterranean did have great effects.

Normally we think of an area in terms of land, but the center of ancient Greece was really a body of water, the blue Aegean Sea, which is an arm of the Mediterranean. What will be called "Greece" in later pages is this sea, the European and Asiatic coasts on either side, and the islands in the middle. Diversity in local ways is encouraged by this physical division, and yet seaborne forces tend to link all parts of this world. Over-all, the region we shall consider as ancient Greece stretched 400 miles from the west coast and islands of mainland Greece to Asia Minor.

On the western, or European, side of the Aegean lies the area forming the modern country of Greece—this is the southern tip of the Balkan peninsula, the southeasternmost extension of Europe. Here the rugged limestone mountains of the Balkan highlands have slipped into the sea. The islands of the Aegean are the peaks of these drowned mountains; long fingers of water extend up into the land and divide it into many small pockets. In the past, volcanic activity was at times violent, and earthquakes still occur frequently.

Mainland Greece is divided almost in two by the Saronic gulf and the Corinthian gulf. Below this dividing line is the Peloponnesus, in which lie Sparta, the hills of Arcadia, the shrine of Olympia, and Argos. The isthmus of Corinth, a narrow neck of land only four miles wide at its narrowest point, joins the Peloponnesus to the rest of mainland Greece. Nowadays the isthmus is pierced by a small canal, but in ancient times ships could be dragged across it on a stone causeway. North of the isthmus were Athens, Thebes (and other cities of the plain of Boeotia), the sanctuary of Delphi, and Thessaly. These names will turn up again and again in the course of Greek history.

North of Thessaly lay the kingdom of Macedonia, which the Greeks considered barbarian—that is, not Greek-speaking and alien in customs. A mountainous divide separated the Mediterranean world from the different vegetation and climate of what is today Yugoslavia and Bulgaria. Even today Greeks talk about "going to Europe" when they take a trip to Paris; their connections lie almost as much with Asia and Africa. On the busy streets of Athens one may see Boy Scouts from Libya side by side with tourists from England and America.

Many islands stud the Aegean, so that on a clear day one is never out of sight of land in crossing from the European shore to the Asiatic shore. Midway is a group of small islands called the Cyclades, grouped around the great religious shrine of Apollo on the little, waterless island of Delos. On the south stretches the long, narrow bulk of Crete. In early times this was the home of the great Minoan culture, but in the historic period Crete played no great role. Just off the Asiatic coast are several fairly large islands, including, from north to south, Lesbos, the home of the poetess Sappho; Chios, which laid claim to being the home of Homer; Samos, the birthplace of the philosopher Pythagoras; and also the island of Rhodes, an important way station on the ancient naval route to the Near East.

The eastern shore of the Aegean is part of Turkey today, but in ancient times the Greeks occupied almost all the coastal plains. These are extensive and are well watered by rivers such as the Hermus and Maeander, which pour down from the central plateau of Asia Minor.

Photo by Harissiadis—Athens
Always in the Greek background are mountains, often with snow.

Many thriving cities on this coast traded inland with the native kingdom of Lydia as well as out to sea.

The climate in the Greek world is called "Mediterranean" and resembles that of southern California. Summers are hot and dry; the winds blow primarily from the Eurasian continent toward the heat-box of the Sahara. Then in the fall, moisture-laden winds push in from the west and rain falls in sudden bursts. The western side of mainland Greece has twice as much moisture as Athens, where the rains begin about November and cease in late April. In fact, most of the rivers in Greece are filled in winter and spring and virtually dry up in the summer.

The Mediterranean Sea serves as a moderating force to the climate, cooling the air in summer and warming it in winter. This moderating influence does not extend far inland, or into the mountains, where snows can lie all winter. Yet along the southern coasts the climate of Greece is really subtropical. Today bananas are grown in various parts of the Peloponnesus, and people can be out of doors much of the year. Even in winter there are many sunny days, and they are mild along the coasts.

Effects of the Environment 🌀🌀🌀🌀🌀🌀🌀🌀🌀🌀🌀🌀🌀🌀🌀🌀🌀🌀🌀🌀🌀
In the Mediterranean climate people need less artificial warmth than do those of us who live where snow is common in winter. Because the weather was usually moderate, and their simple houses had no attractions to keep the ancient Greeks indoors, they tended to associate together in a hubbub of activity during waking hours. Also, sources of water that flowed constantly were so few that the Greeks lived close together in villages built near springs, rather than in scattered farm houses, and thus could congregate easily.

Still, each little island was separated from its neighbors by the sea, and in mainland Greece mountain ridges carved the landscape into tiny plains. Today we think of "Greece" as a country with a blue and white flag, but in ancient times Greece was divided into more independent states than exist anywhere in the modern world. No one even dreamed of their being united into a single political unit. Athens, Sparta, Corinth, and a host of other "countries" had very different forms of government and ways of life even though they shared a common language and social customs and gathered with other states at great religious shrines.

Another major characteristic was simplicity of life. A Spartan king once said, "In Greece poverty has always been our companion." True, many parts of Greece had simple but essential raw materials, such as good clay for making pots, marble, and other building stones; there was copper on the island of Euboea, iron and lead in Sparta, silver in Athens; but the basic occupation in ancient times was farming, and this produced very small surpluses. In looking at ancient Greece we shall be observing some of the most important political and intellectual problems of man in an almost primitive setting.

Historically the position of the Aegean world was of great importance, for it lay halfway between barbarian Europe and the original seats of civilization in the Near East. Nomads could trudge down from the European continent across the Balkan mountains to the sea, but could go no farther unless they got ships. Advanced techniques and skills could be brought from the Near East to the

Aegean, but again could not easily be carried across the mountains into Europe.

Consequently the Aegean shores and islands were the first parts of Europe to become civilized in ancient times. The great centers of Greek culture, such as Athens, Corinth, and Miletus, lay in the parts of Greece which were most open to influences from the Near East.

How the Greeks Made Their Living

Most of us do not know very much about the sources of our food; the phrase "earning a living" as often refers to luxuries as to the essentials of life· Almost all ancient Greeks on the other hand had to think first and last of getting enough to eat, and nearly every inhabitant of Greece belonged to a farming family.

Nowadays one farmer in the United States can support 42½ people who do not raise their own food and fibers (up from 15½ in 1950!). For ancient Greece there are no such precise statistics, but 6 farmers were probably required to produce enough surplus for 1 non-farmer. Crop yields were almost incredibly low, and the Greek technique of farming, which is discussed below (see page 18), demanded a great deal of human physical labor. So most Greeks lived in agricultural villages, which had populations of anywhere from several hundred to a few thousand people.

Within these villages some farmers held much more land than others, and there were landless men who made a miserable existence doing day work during the busier seasons. Slaves could be bought to work the land, but they were not a very profitable rural investment because agricultural yields were so low. In Thessaly, Sparta, and Crete, however, many or most of the small farmers were bound to their plots and had to make fixed payments to lords. Everywhere men struggled with primitive tools to raise the food, thus permitting a few thinkers to develop the higher levels of Greek civilization.

Although the "average Greek" was a sunburned man wrestling with the soil by hand tools, ancient writers had little interest in such a humdrum figure. Insofar as ordinary people appear in Greek literature, it is usually city-dwellers who engaged in commerce and industry. These people are important to us, too, for the craftsmen and artisans were the men who made the artistic products of ancient Greece, and the merchants spread Greek civilization throughout the Mediterranean.

This coin of Zankle (modern Messina
in Sicily) shows its natural harbor,
with a dolphin inside. It is one
of the first surviving Greek maps.

No part of European or Asiatic Greece was more than a day or
two from the coasts, and the islanders lived with water all about
them. Ports were easily available for the small ships; navigation was
relatively simple in areas where a sailor was never far from sight of
land. From prehistoric times a few inhabitants of the Aegean were
driven to use the sea, though only in the summer, when travel was
safest. The ships used in commerce were extremely small vessels,
and carried scarcely more than 80 tons of cargo in pots or other containers. Sometimes they were rowed, for galleys could move inde-
pendently of the winds; but galleys were used mainly in warfare.
The main type of war galley was the trireme, which was propelled
by 150 rowers, 75 on either side arranged in groups of three which
were staggered inboard. Sailing craft were broader and deeper, and
usually had on one mast a square sail made of hides or linen, with
sometimes a little sail on a foremast. Like the galleys, the sailing craft
could be run up on a sandy beach, though natural or artificial harbors
became steadily more important as commerce developed.

The sailing craft carried bold Greek merchants from Cadiz, on the
Atlantic coast of Spain, to the coasts of Syria in the east; north to
the Black Sea and the Russian Crimea; and south to Egypt and
Libya. Eventually a network of Greek colonies developed which
provided safe ports to merchants and also spread Greek culture inland into the continent of Europe. From the western Mediterranean
and the Black Sea, merchants gained primarily raw materials (copper, tin, wool, dried fish, wheat, and the like) and slaves. These the
Greeks either used themselves or sold in the civilized ports of the
Near East. Such manufactured luxuries as ointments and perfumes,
ivory objects, metal products, and paper (made from papyrus stems
in Egypt) came from the Near East to Greece, and sometimes were
carried on to the west and north.

Borrowing techniques and skills from the more advanced Near
East, the Greeks developed their own manufactures and added a

Photo by Harissiadis—Athens

Aegean Shipping

War galleys were long and slim. On the prow was a ram, often decorated with an eye to help the ship see where it was going. On either side of the stern were large steering oars, for the rudder was not known in ancient times. While cruising, a galley could use a sail on its central mast (see the galley on page 31); in this case the rowers are also at their seats, oars out. This galley is an early type (not a trireme), so the rowers are not in groups of three. (Like many illustrations on later pages, this is from an ancient vase-painting.)

Modern sailing caiques in the Aegean are very much like the little sailing craft in which the ancient Greeks boldly traversed the Mediterranean.

distinctive style, which eventually made Greek pottery, metalwork, statues, and textiles popular on all the Mediterranean shores. Vases produced in one Athenian workshop about 510 B.C. have been found in south Russia, Etruria (north of Rome), and Egypt. Scuba divers and underseas explorers have discovered in recent years many wrecks of ancient vessels which had been carrying loads ranging from ingots of copper, statuary, and architectural stonework to pottery jars (originally containing wine or olive oil).

Industry to us means huge factories with power-driven machines and specialized labor. In ancient Greece everything was made by hand or at the most with the use of simple hand tools. One man might shape, another decorate, and a third fire a vase; but specialization scarcely proceeded further. Most artisans worked in shops that employed only a very few people. Neither animal nor wind power was used in industry; to increase production the best means was to buy a slave.

At one point there were more than 20,000 slaves in Athens and its silver mines. Some of the slaves were Greek, but most came from barbarian tribes. Legally slaves were property, and in the mines suffered a dismal, short existence; but in the cities they seem to have lived much as the poorer citizens did and sometimes were given responsible positions. The police of Athens, for example, were Scythian archers, state slaves bought in south Russia.

Free or slave, in city or country, most men worked hard with their bodies and wore themselves out quickly. When a man fell sick or became old, he had only his family or close friends to care for him, for society had little surplus to support non-workers. An ancient Greek usually died by the age of 35. Women's life expectancy was even less because of the risks and frequency of childbearing. The death rate of babies was extremely high.

Nonetheless, ancient Greece had an expanding population, which managed to wrest enough food from the soil for itself in most regions. The more prosperous areas along the seacoasts could afford to import wheat, especially as trade and industry developed. In these districts small farming villages eventually became real cities. Of the states mentioned in earlier pages, all but Sparta had true urban centers. Athens, probably the largest city in ancient Greece, may have had 150,000 residents at its height, but this was possible only because wheat could be shipped from the north Aegean and south Russia to its busy port of Piraeus.

Hand Work in Ancient Greece

On the one vase, the shoemaker, seated on a simple stool, is cutting leather for a pair of shoes; samples and tools are shown, suspended from the wall. On the other vase, which shows a bronze foundry, there is more specialization. One man tends a furnace on the left, while a boy pumps the bellows behind; on the right a statue is being assembled. Here also tools appear on the wall.

This statue of Apollo from Olympia is one of the greatest illustrations of a Greek god. Endowed with eternal strength, Apollo is calmly stretching out his arm to stop a fierce battle (which is being fought on either side of him); clearly, men of his age believed in his power.

The Religious Spirit 𓂀𓂀𓂀𓂀𓂀𓂀𓂀𓂀𓂀𓂀𓂀𓂀𓂀𓂀𓂀𓂀𓂀𓂀𓂀𓂀𓂀

In such uncertain and brief lives men could not dare to feel themselves masters of their own destinies. Particularly with regard to the success of their crops, their animals, and their own reproduction, ancient Greeks had to think religiously in cases where we today would think scientifically; for forces outside their control and comprehension brought war or peace, strong or sickly babies, plague or good health. Since these forces were of many different kinds, the Greeks felt that there must be many gods too, each having a specialized function with regard to men and to nature.

Some gods formed the group of great deities who lived on the top of Mount Olympus (the highest mountain in Greece) under the general control of Father Zeus (see page 24). Others, however, were local gods for a particular state or smaller area of land. In addition, each family had its patron spirits. Marriage was essentially a matter of introducing a new woman into the care of those spirits, for they controlled each major stage of human life from birth through puberty to death.

Through dreams, the flight of birds, and unusual natural phenomena the gods could reveal their will to man. At some great religious shrines one could consult a god through a priest or priestess and receive an oracle. Usually this advice was ambiguous and could be interpreted to fit the way things did turn out.

Essentially the Greeks were optimistic enough to believe that the divine forces were at the least neutral toward man. There were evil spirits, but in Greek religion there was no devil. To make the gods favorable one offered the proper prayers and sacrifices of animals, wheat cakes, or other agricultural products. Officials called "priests" did this for the state as a whole, and the father sacrificed for his family. Much of the religious activity was conducted in public on behalf of groups, not individuals.

Into all aspects of life the Greeks interwove a deeply religious spirit to a degree which most of us today would find hard to understand. The drama, both tragic and comic, was directly connected with festivals of the god Dionysus at Athens; and much of the earliest poetry was composed to be sung at religious ceremonies. Virtually all sculpture down to the 5th century B.C. was erected in religious sites, and the major buildings of any community were its temples. In art as in daily life, Greek religion was essentially sane and encouraging, and it was a dominant force.

Summary.   Thus far we have looked at the background of the Greeks geographically, economically, and religiously. When one meets a stranger, it always helps to know as much as one can about where he comes from, where he went to school, and what kind of job he has before trying to judge his opinions or to understand why he acts as he does.

The manner of living of the ancient Greeks was so simple that most of us would consider it primitive; some aspects of their religious and superstitious outlooks would strike us as backward, even for a caveman. Also, their communities and political units were extremely small in scale, as were their buildings—compare, for example, the Parthenon and a modern skyscraper. But as this comparison may suggest, great things do not necessarily come in large packages. A clear knowledge of the simplicity of the Greek background throws into a more vivid light the tremendous achievements and lasting influence of the civilization which the Greeks created.

Rural Life

**Gods and
Superstitions
in Greece**

Greek Athletics

RURAL LIFE

Most Greek literature was written by men who lived in cities and belonged to the aristocracy. So in the poems and plays there is little of the rural ways of life, and it is easy to forget the importance of agriculture until one looks, for example, at the coins which the many Greek states struck in profusion. Normally these bear on one side an image of the patron deity of the state; on the reverse there is often an ear of wheat, a bunch of grapes, a bull, a sheep, or other reference to the agricultural basis of life.

Actually nearly all Greeks spent their years from childhood to old age in the annual round of agricultural work. Since crops were weeded and harvested by hand, a farmer and his family could scarcely cultivate more than 2 or 3 acres in any one season; and the absence of modern fertilizers forced him to leave part of his land uncultivated each year so that it could regain its fertility.

One poet, Hesiod, does tell us a good deal about farming.* Hesiod, who lived in Boeotia about 700 B.C., had a dispute with his brother Perses over their father's estate and was cheated by "bribe-swallowing" judges. His anger led him to write a great poem in Homeric style, the

* Hesiod is pronounced He-se-od. The pronunciation of unusual Greek words is given in the Glossary.

wheat   grape   bull   cock

Agriculture on Greek Coins

Works and Days, the aim of which was to show that the gods punished injustice and that the right way to prosper was to be a good farmer.

Hesiod described the agricultural calendar as beginning just before the fall rains, for the climate of Greece required a winter cycle of agriculture rather than the summer cycle to which we are accustomed. This fact, incidentally, meant that in Greek warfare, men generally fought only in the summer, when they otherwise would have been idle; in the fall they returned home to plant their crops.

According to Hesiod, however, the farmer broke the soil in a spring or summer ploughing, and he ploughed a second, final time in the fall. Greek ploughs were simple wooden tools, the bottom of which was possibly tipped with iron, pulled by oxen, and they did little more than break the thin soils. Behind the plough a member of the farmer's family or a slave cut the clods with hoes or other tools, likewise mostly wooden, and hid the scattered seed of wheat or barley from the birds. As the farmer began this fall ploughing, Hesiod urged prayers especially to Zeus and to Demeter, goddess of the grain.

Throughout the winter and spring there were other religious ceremonies to protect the growing crops. During these seasons farmers weeded their fields by hand. At the harvest season in May, everyone who could work labored from dawn to dark to cut the ripe grain with sickles, for the time was short in which to gather the sheaves at just the right point. Grain was threshed on stone threshing floors by oxen, which were driven around and around to separate the wheat from the chaff. Although we cannot estimate yields accurately, farmers in Athens probably harvested about half of the meager crops which can be raised there today. In the last months before the harvest, "things grow but a man cannot eat his fill," as a Greek poet put it; short rations must have been common in these anxious months. Still, the climate and the simple methods of agriculture were in general good enough to prevent serious famines.

In addition to wheat and barley on the flat lands, farmers cultivated on the hillsides olive trees and vines, which could live during the dry summer because they had roots that grew deep enough to reach moist ground. Olive and grape harvests were in early fall and were also accompanied by religious ceremonies. When the new wine was ready to drink in late winter-early spring, great celebrations were carried out in honor of Dionysus, god of wine. Other foodstuffs included vegetables such as beans and peas, which were sometimes raised in small irrigated plots; nuts, figs, and apples; and honey from the bees which buzzed among the fragrant thyme and other scrub growth of the hillsides.

The Greeks also raised animals, but with some difficulty. Sheep and goats were most common, for they could be pastured on the hills (where they helped to deforest the slopes). Pigs were driven into the forests (where available) to eat acorns. Oxen and horses, however, required winter forage, which was not easily obtained. (Hesiod advises a farmer to cut their rations in half in winter.) Oxen drew ploughs and

The Time of Ploughing and Sowing
(another example of the simple Greek plough will be found in the picture on page 145)

British Museum

The Time of Harvesting
(threshing in the old fashion took place in Greece until recently)

wagons; horses were raised only by the well-to-do and then principally for racing and for war. The horse collar was not developed until the end of ancient times as a way of harnessing horse power effectively.

Rural life, as pictured by Hesiod, was hard. In one line he insists, "work with work upon work." It was also a cautious world. Hesiod urges his listeners never to make agreements without witnesses; as for women, "the man who trusts womankind trusts deceivers." Toward a neighbor who begged for food one might be generous once or twice, but after that the neighbor must hunger.

Yet farming life had its moments of relaxation. In summer, if the farmer was not fighting, he could sit in the shade, his face turned toward a fresh breeze, and drink wine; in winter, the crowded smithy tempted the lazy farmer to while away his time with friends. In the early days especially, the hunting of wild boar or deer was a common

Olive Trees

Olive trees grow well in the thin red soils of Greece, both on the plains and on the hillsides; they have been cultivated since prehistoric times. It takes as much as 15 years for an olive grove to be profitable, but then the gnarled trees can bear for centuries. The vase-painting shows harvesting, with one man up in the tree and others beating the branches. (A comparison of the trees in the two pictures will suggest that Greek artists were not worried about showing nature as it really is.)

as well as useful sport protected by the divine huntress Artemis, but later the wild animals were driven far back into the hills by the spread of civilization. Athletic contests continued to take place, however, often at religious festivals.

The village communities were tightly woven, but simple, social structures bound together by religion. Apart from the great gods, who were worshipped in temples, every village felt itself encircled and guarded by divine spirits. The god Hermes, patron of wayfarers, was thought to live in the stone piles heaped by the side of the roads; fountains and springs had their nymphs; forests were populated by satyrs and silens, half-human, half-animal. On the hills and mountains lived spirits called muses, and those of Mount Helicon taught Hesiod how to be a poet. In fact, reverence to the divine forces which governed and aided man's work is prominent throughout his *Works and Days*.

A huntsman comes home with
two rabbits on a stick, his
dog jumping up beside him.

GODS AND SUPERSTITIONS IN GREECE

Religion was a very important cement in Greek society. This religious spirit existed on many different levels; the most sublime faith stood beside the grossest of superstition.

When most of us think of Greek religion, we probably remember scandalous stories of Greek mythology or perhaps the way the gods maneuver the heroes of Homer's *Iliad* and *Odyssey*. This might be called the international or literary level of Greek religion. As the historian Herodotus observed, "Homer and Hesiod set the form of the gods" for all the Greeks; but we must remember too that a philosopher (Xenophanes) could burst out in anger, "Homer and Hesiod have ascribed to the gods all things that are a shame and a disgrace among mortals, stealings, adulteries, and deceivings of one another." For the gods who lived on Mount Olympus were visualized as human in their passions and loves, but also as divine inasmuch as they had superhuman powers and could not be killed.

Eventually the Greeks singled out 12 of these greater gods as most important. Zeus (1) was the sky god, the master over all, whose only limitation was that he could not undo the decisions of abstract Fate. His sister-wife was Hera (2), who protected marriage. His brother, Poseidon (3), controlled the seas in historic times but earlier had been conceived as bringer of earthquakes and deity of horses. Zeus' sisters were Hestia (4), goddess of the hearth, and Demeter (5), who had

Ancestral Traditions

Not all the Greek views of the divine were expressed in terms of the gods of Homer. From the Dark Ages on, there are crude pictures of a female figure who controls nature and holds panthers and deer by their necks; this powerful force does not turn up at all in Homer, and is called by modern scholars "The Mistress of Wild Animals." Here she is shown on a 6th-century vase; note her ornate robe (*peplos*).

In primitive societies dancing is very often connected with religious celebrations. Grotesque masks of clay which were worn by such dancers in early Greece have been found; in this scene men wear bulls' heads and tails. Perhaps they are pretending to be Minotaurs (the mythical figure, half-man, half-bull, who lurked in the Labyrinth at Cnossus and ate young men and women until Theseus killed him).

Greek National Tourist Office

One of the most majestic sites any religion has ever created is the shrine of Apollo at Delphi. A deep gorge slashes below the sanctuary down to the Corinthian gulf; great rocks tower overhead. All major Greek states erected trophies or buildings at Delphi, even though the stones had to be hauled several miles up the mountainside from the sea. The temple of Apollo, the home of his greatest oracle, was rebuilt several times. When the site was excavated by French archeologists, they moved the whole modern village of Delphi and then cleared off the mounds of huge rocks which had fallen from the cliffs. In this view the theater is in the foreground; some surviving columns of the temple of Apollo can be seen just beyond.

given grain to man and protected women in their troubles. Of Zeus' many children, Athena (6) had sprung fully armed from his head; Athena was patroness of arts and crafts, but at Athens she was also a war goddess. Zeus had twins by the mortal maid Leto, Apollo (7), the god of wisdom, and Artemis (8), deity of the wild. Other children were Ares (9), god of war; Aphrodite (10), goddess of love; Hermes (11), messenger and also patron of wayfarers; Hephaestus (12), who was lame and served as smith to the gods.

Some of these gods had been worshipped, as we shall see later,

This head of a bronze statue of Zeus (or perhaps Poseidon) was found years ago in the sea off Cape Artemisium. It is one of the greatest sculptures of the 5th century. For another great conception of a Greek god, see the head of Apollo on page 14.

since the period before 1200 B.C.; but Greek religion was ever changing. It never was set down in a sacred book; the priests who carried out sacrifices were essentially public officials and were not believed to have special powers. As the Greeks began to think more consciously about religion, their philosophers elevated Zeus higher and higher; the other gods continued to exist. Beside the major divinities, revered all over Greece, there were the many gods who had special functions or exercised power over a local district or family. On a lower plane were the heroes, men who had performed great deeds and were worshipped at their graves as protectors of the community. One of these mortals, Heracles, was actually admitted to Mount Olympus.

Apart from local festivals in honor of heroes or the gods of the state, international celebrations developed at Olympia, the isthmus of Corinth, Delphi, Delos, and elsewhere. Great poets and orators often commanded a wide audience at the festivals, but the main events were usually athletic competitions (see page 33). Everywhere, however, there were shrines at which one could make offerings; often these were clay figurines, which women dedicated by the thousands at shrines of Demeter.

Religion was a force which encouraged the Greeks in the arts, letters, and athletics in its public manifestations, but a great amount of superstition, magic, and emotionalism also persisted throughout their history. Women were considered "unclean" during menstrual periods and after childbirth; babies were protected by magic tokens, such as amulets; an enemy was cursed if one inscribed evil wishes on a lead plate and buried it in the ground. The poet Hesiod tells us which days of the month were good and bad for various activities, and he warns his listener that when one buys a cooking pot it must be taken straightaway to the village magician to be blessed. Human sacrifice was practiced as a fertility rite in the backward hills of Arcadia after the time of the birth of Christ. At Athens in the time of Pericles, two human beings, a male and a female, were driven out of the city each year at a spring festival just before the harvest. Quite possibly these scapegoats, who bore on their shoulders the sins of the community, were stoned to death.

Corpses were interred with appropriate ceremonies, which often involved funeral feasts and the burial·of food, jewelry, and other valuables in the grave. Dead persons were generally believed to stay in their graves, and archeologists have found "feeding tubes" through which wine could be poured to the vicinity of the mouth. At certain times their ghosts did leave their graves for a while to wander on earth,

Staatliche Museen, Berlin

On a high-backed couch sit a dead man and his wife. The husband holds a drinking cup, the wife stretches out her hands. Before them, and much smaller, are the children, who offer a cock, flowers, and other tokens to the dead. Behind the couch is a huge snake, a symbol of earth and the underworld; in ancient times the snake did not have the unpleasant reputation it does today. This relief, from Chrysapha near Sparta, was carved by a small-town sculptor just after 550 B.C.; a much more sophisticated gravestone, carved 200 years later, is shown on page 43.

however, and they had to be appeased by magic rites (compare our Halloween). Another line of thought separated a soul from the body. Some Greeks did believe in reincarnation, others believed in the Isles of the Blest, and still others visualized a dim underworld, Hades, in which gray souls sadly wandered. Life on this earth was what counted most, so that the important life after death was a matter of being remembered by one's sons. As Electra said to her father Agamemnon, "When a man dies, children are the voice of his salvation afterward."

In every state the calendar was marked by an extensive set of religious ceremonies. Every great public sacrifice brought with it an emotional sense of unity with the deity who was being worshipped. The god received a part of the animal victim, which was burned on the large altar in front of his temple, and the people participating in the ceremony ate the rest (one of the rare times when they ate meat). There were, however, secret ceremonies into which one had to be initiated, like the "mysteries" of Eleusis in honor of Demeter, which were celebrated there every year for over 1000 years. Some Greeks even belonged to closed religious circles which believed they had a special revelation. Among these were the Orphics, who claimed the legendary musician-god Orpheus as their guide to eternal salvation.

The most common emotional release came in the worship of the god Dionysus, patron of wine, who was attended by reeling male satyrs and dancing female maenads. Sometimes both sexes engaged in Dionysiac revels; often the women of a community engaged in their own separate rites. In Euripides' tragedy, the *Bacchae*, the females of Thebes tore off the head of the king who intruded on their nocturnal worship of Dionysus, and the king's own mother bore it triumphantly back to the city. By the 6th and 5th centuries B.C. political leaders were trying

Bank Leu

Hundreds of coins and vases depict Dionysus. This is a magnificent close-up of his head, with ivy wreath, from Naxos in Sicily.

Dionysus the Great

Both these vases were painted in the mid-6th century at Athens. One, by the great master Exekias, shows the bearded Dionysus sailing across a magic sea. A vine laden with grapes grows out of the ship; dolphins cavort about.

The other, by Amasis (who put his name above the scene), illustrates Dionysus with a great drinking cup. Two richly robed maenads dance up to Dionysus; one offers a rabbit, the other has a panther skin.

31

desperately to limit and to civilize festivals of Dionysus; as already observed, at Athens this effort led to the development of drama.

Greek religion thus offered many outlets for the stresses and fears of life. At one extreme stood the god Apollo, whose priests at Delphi preached moderation and self-knowledge as the key to wise living. At the other extreme were the liberating ecstasies of Dionysus. So too each of us today can turn now to rational, now to emotional, releases for our problems and tensions.

The Greeks were far too earth-centered, keen of thought, and materially successful in their great days to yield themselves utterly to religious preoccupations, however clearly they recognized human frailty. Yet both as individuals and as members of various groups they shared in a rich religious pattern. Much of their religion remained primitive, for it was crystallized early amid a simple folk. The picturesque Homeric view of the gods as being numerous and as sharing all basic human qualities could never be removed, even though a great philosopher was later to emphasize that "there is one god, among gods and men the greatest, not at all like mortals in body or in mind." The most practical test of religion, however, is perhaps whether it consoles and inspirits men in their daily battles with the world. The many strands of Greek faith satisfied this test on the level of the individual, of the family and clan, and of the state. Above all, Greek religion had an optimistic, confident quality which rose above gross superstition and fostered the continued development of the arts and letters.

GREEK ATHLETICS

Every four years the great international Olympic games, which were revived in 1896, serve as a direct reminder of an important side of Greek life. Athletics turns up everywhere in Greek literature and art, partly because the aristocratic way of life heavily stressed physical prowess.

The great Greek contests occurred every four years at Olympia and Delphi (Pythian games) and every two years at the isthmus of Corinth (Isthmian games) and Nemea. The Olympic games, the most famous, began with one day of racing and wrestling and, according to tradition, were first celebrated in 776 B.C. In the 7th century B.C. chariot-racing and single-horse races were added, and by the 5th century the religious ceremonies and contests for boys and men spread over five days. The winners received only crowns of wild olive leaves, but when they returned home they were escorted into their city with great pomp. Sometimes a hole was pierced in the city wall for their special entry. A victor might even be given meals at state expense for his lifetime.

International and local contests were almost always connected with religious festivals. Such contests took place in stadiums. Many Greek cities developed gymnasiums, where men of leisure could engage in less formal athletics. A gymnasium was a plot of ground on the edge of town, partly open land, partly a grove of trees. Often it had baths, so that men could scrub themselves and then oil their bodies to protect them against the parching Greek sun.

Running was always the chief contest. The list of Olympic victors in the sprint or *stadium* race (about 200 yards) was a famous guide to chronology. But chariot-racing, which could be afforded only by the rich, came to be the equivalent of modern automobile races in its popularity.

Greek National Tourist Office

Even to climb up to the stadium at Delphi exhausts a modern tourist, for it lies high above the temple and theater area. The original starting grooves for runners can still be seen at one end.

There is a story that in one early Olympic race a runner's shorts fell off and he went on to win the race, so that thereafter all competitors raced nude. Both at the games and in the gymnasiums sculptors and vase-painters became well acquainted with the nude male body in action or in repose. Only at Sparta, however, did girls take part in regular athletic contests.

Although simple ball games existed, most Greek athletics involved individual competition, such as boxing, wrestling, discus-throwing, javelin-hurling, broad-jumping, and running. Races were run either in armor or in the nude. Some races were short, some long. Boys competed with boys, and men with men of the same age. The aristocratic ideal in the gymnasium was to show good form, but the drive to win occasionally produced scandals of bribery and deceit in ancient Olympic games just as it has in their modern successors.

These are two sides of a sculptured base which was built into the wall that the Athenians hastily erected after the Persian invasion. On the left side of the wrestlers a youth is in the usual position to start running; on the right another is testing his javelin. The second side shows a ball game played with curved sticks.

CHAPTER 2

The Rise of Athens to Greatness

Dates and History ▨▨▨▨▨▨▨▨▨▨▨▨▨▨▨▨▨▨▨▨▨▨▨▨▨▨
Down to this point there have been almost no dates. Students of history often grumble about having to learn dates, and in truth there is no magic significance to any historical date in itself. Whether Columbus discovered America in 1492, 1491, or 1493, for example, is rather incidental. What *is* important is that the New World and the Old World became linked after the Renaissance was under way and the modern states of Europe (such as England, Spain, and France) had begun to emerge and to engage in rivalries.

If we drive far along a highway without signposts, we feel very uncomfortable and unsure of our way. For historians, dates are signposts used to show the relation of one event to another. In the opening pages we were looking at some enduring factors in Greek history, factors which had lasting influence on its development, and so dates were not very necessary.

In history, however, there is always change as well as continuity. From now on, accordingly, dates will be used as pegs for the major marks of that change.*

---

* All dates will be B.C. unless otherwise noted. To find how long 440 B.C. was before A.D. 1960, for example, one must *add* the two figures: the answer is 2400 years ago. We do not know the precise dates for many ancient figures; the best estimates are given in the Glossary after the person's name. Time charts will be found in each major section of this book; a summary time chart, No. 7, is on page 176.

Human inhabitation of the Aegean shores extends back to the earliest ages of man, but the first great examples of civilization are the Minoan and Mycenaean cultures of the 2d millennium (2000–1000 B.C.). Then came a wave of invasions. The invaders wiped out those earlier cultures and paved the way for the evolution of the intellectual, political, and artistic way of life which we call "Greek."

True Greek civilization developed slowly in the centuries after 1000 B.C., but not until just before 700 B.C. did it begin its great period of expansion and consolidation. The height of what we term "Classic" Greece came in the 5th century B.C. (The 5th century B.C. is the period of the 400's before Christ, just as the 20th century after Christ is the 1900's.)

The first part of this book will consider the rise of Greek civilization, and the second part its subsequent expansion after Alexander the Great. What we are going to do, however, is different from the way a historian usually operates. Frequently a history starts at the beginning of its period and proceeds in grimly chronological fashion to the end of the story; but we shall jump into the middle and stay there for quite a while. That is to say, we shall now travel to Athens in about the year 440 B.C. to look at the main characteristics of Greek civilization as they appeared at that one spot and time. Then we can turn back to see how the Greek way of life had developed before 440, and also find out what happened thereafter.

The Greatness of Athens

In the 5th century B.C. the Greek world consisted of hundreds of independent countries. Some of these were as large or as powerful as Athens, and in earlier centuries several of them had been more important in art and literature than Athens. By 440, however, Athens was becoming the center of Greek civilization. What was taking place in this bustling urban life was one of the greatest political and cultural outbursts of all time.

At home Athens had developed the most complete democracy Greece ever produced; in some ways it is true that no later government has been more democratic. Abroad the Athenians had developed a sea-based mastery over much of the Aegean so as to form the first great empire in Greek history. Its port of Piraeus was the center of Aegean trade, which was largely carried on in terms of Athenian currency; the red-figured vases of Athenian potters dominated Mediterranean taste. For the first time in history a state now appeared

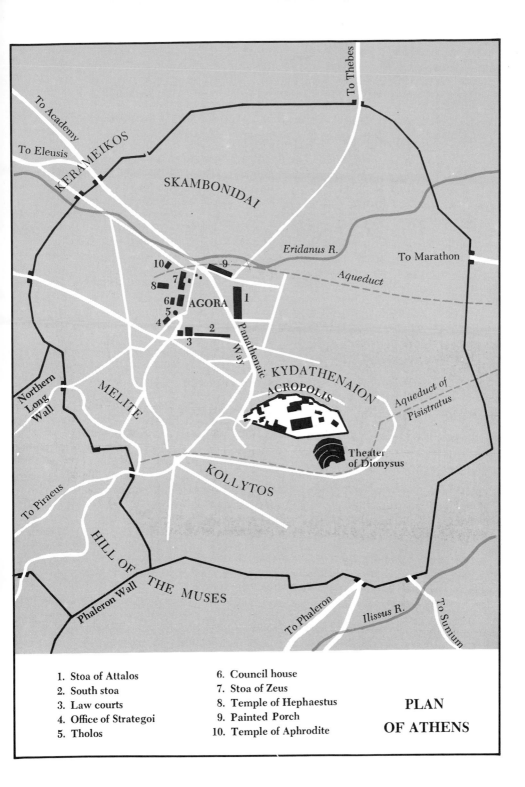

1. Stoa of Attalos
2. South stoa
3. Law courts
4. Office of Strategoi
5. Tholos
6. Council house
7. Stoa of Zeus
8. Temple of Hephaestus
9. Painted Porch
10. Temple of Aphrodite

PLAN

OF ATHENS

that could not feed its citizens from its own lands, for Periclean Athens became so large and so specialized in economic activity that its farms could not provide the city-dwellers with enough grain.

Philosophers, men of letters, and artists were drawn to this center of Greece just as traders were. For example, the "Father of History," Herodotus of Halicarnassus, went there after traveling over much of the Near East and the Black Sea, marveling at the Pyramids in Egypt or the Hanging Gardens of Babylon; at Athens he recited his great story of the rise of the Persian empire and its defeat by the Greeks. Most of the men, however, who were making Athens an eternal synonym for culture were native-born.

In and around the marketplace (Agora), temples, covered walkways (*stoas*), and other buildings were rising, but the greatest edifice, which still serves as *the* symbol of ancient Greek genius, was on the great rock of the Acropolis above; the Parthenon was almost finished by 440. On the south slope of the Acropolis was the theater of Dionysus, where the great tragedian Aeschylus had put on his plays. In 440 Aeschylus was dead, but Euripides had just gained his first prize for tragedy and Sophocles was still active. Soon a much younger man, Aristophanes, would begin to present lively comedies here. A bulb-nosed critic of life who "did nothing but persuade you men of Athens to take thought first for your own souls" was always about; he was the famous Socrates. Presiding over both the political and cultural life of Athens was its reserved and severe, but highly cherished, leader of democracy, Pericles.

Daily Life of a Citizen

This self-confident people was born, as one of its foreign enemies said, "never to have peace nor to allow others to have peace." To see how they lived, let us put ourselves in the place of an ordinary citizen of Athens, whom we shall call Cleon.

Although Greek sculptors created idealized types of human bodies, in reality a man like Cleon was short, swarthy, and weather-hardened. So too his outlook on life was not idealistic or sentimental but brutally frank; he was inclined to quick anger. In terms of housing, dress, and food, Cleon was below the poverty level of today.

His house was a simple box without heating or plumbing, made of sun-dried brick which was plastered to protect it from the rains. Light came from an interior court, for there were no windows on the

A young woman in a *peplos* robe, barefoot, is putting away folded clothes in an ornate chest. The chest is decorated with a <u>meander</u> or <u>Greek-key pattern</u> and also figured scenes from Greek mythology (on the left a goddess is subduing a giant). Behind her is an armchair with cushions. On the wall are a basket, mirror with handle, jug, and drinking cup.

ground floor (robbers had to break through the walls, which was not difficult). If there was an upper story, it was reached by a ladder and was assigned to the women. Furniture was expensive and very limited; rich people at least had simple chairs and boxes or chests for storage. They also had a "men's quarters" or dining room equipped with sofas with cord webbing, on which diners reclined behind little tables. Each family had its shrine of Hestia, goddess of the hearth, and other family gods, who were revered daily but more specially on major anniversaries.

Food was cooked on a simple brazier or charcoal grill. For breakfast Cleon would eat some very coarse bread dipped in wine; his lunch would be little more extensive. Dinner, which Cleon ate at the close of the day, consisted of a few vegetables such as beans, peas, onions, and turnips; fish or, as a delicacy, eel; apples, figs, and more bread. Olive oil was the primary fat; honey was virtually the only source of sugar. Meat would be eaten principally at great sacrifices, especially lambs in the spring. Wine was preserved in containers smeared with pitch to make them watertight. Usually this wine was so strong that it was cut with water for drinking; a common ratio was one part of wine to three parts of water.

Cleon's clothing was made almost exclusively from wool. The rich could have linen (cotton and silk were as yet unknown). Both men and women wore clothing which hung from the shoulders. One basic form, the *peplos,* was a long rectangular blanket put about the body and pinned at the shoulders; a more modish dress, the *chiton,* was sewn at the shoulders and often down the sides so as to resemble a nightshirt. In cold weather the more delicate could also add a *himation* or shawl. In town Cleon wore shoes as a protection against the garbage and other waste products of the houses which were thrown into the streets to be washed away in the rains; hats were not town garb, but for the unbroken sunshine of the countryside.

Throughout this life, masculine dominance by Cleon and his friends was obvious. Only men could vote or have legal rights. The women of the more respectable families scarcely went out by themselves, and even Cleon probably did most of the marketing in the Agora as well as loitering at the barber's or the perfumer's. The job of women was to spin wool, tend the home, and raise children. Boys were much preferred; girl babies were sometimes taken to the city gates and "exposed"—left to the mercy of any passerby who might be willing to pick them up.

Athenian writers of the time, like Hesiod long before, often expressed masculine arrogance and suspicion of women. The 4th-century writer Xenophon proposed that men should not marry until 30, after they had had time to sow abundant wild oats, but women should marry at 15; and he lovingly imagined a scene where such a child-wife turned to her husband and exclaimed, "All depends on you."

These pictures of feminine subjection did not entirely correspond to reality, for in the actual course of Athenian life women exercised a significant, and not always hidden, influence. In the tragedies great female figures play mighty roles. In a roaring comedy, *Lysistrata,* Aristophanes has the women of Athens get together and deny themselves to their men until they make peace with Sparta.

Yet it was true at Athens, as in much of the rest of Greece, that men associated with one another to the exclusion of women to a degree not common in modern times. Their endless talking in the

This is the gravestone of Hegeso, which was set up by her husband Proxenos outside the Dipylon Gate of Athens. The solemnity of death has rarely been more ennobled than on these Attic gravestones; they also suggest that husbands could bear deep love for their wives.

Alison Frantz

Agora and elsewhere undoubtedly revolved about scandal and business to a large degree, but there they gained the information which made it possible for them to take part in Athenian democracy. Their vigorous enthusiasm—along with inherited prejudices—both nourished and criticized the great achievements of their playwrights, artists, and philosophers.

The Greek Polis 🏛🏛🏛🏛🏛🏛🏛🏛🏛🏛🏛🏛🏛🏛🏛🏛🏛🏛🏛🏛🏛🏛🏛🏛🏛🏛
Cleon probably left his home soon after breakfast and stayed away all the morning. Each day the narrow, twisting, dirty streets of Athens began to resound with noise and bustle as soon as the sun

Elementary Education

If Cleon had children, the boys were probably taught to read and to write. Their mathematics would have been limited, partly because the Greeks had a poor number system; but music and athletics were very important. Cleon had to pay the expenses of the private teacher, for there were no state schools. Education was largely a matter of rote learning well pounded in by floggings; a school (which was simply a rented room) was a noisy neighbor. Girls were usually taught at home in domestic arts, especially spinning and weaving.

A master is instructing a student on the lyre on the left. Another master holds an open roll for reading (the Greeks did not have bound books). Its opening line has the Greek words *Moisa moi* ("Muse, me . . .), the beginning of a poem by a 6th-century author. Behind the student is a pedagogue, a slave who guarded the youth on the streets and aided his moral education. On the other side of the cup, not shown here, students are playing the double oboe and writing on waxed wooden tablets with styluses. The cup was painted by Duris, a famous red-figure vase painter, early in the 5th century.

rose, and life throbbed until the sun set again. Cleon might have gone to work in a small shop or factory, for most Athenian citizens had to labor in order to earn their livelihood; but unlike most modern men Cleon also played an active, direct role in the government of his country.

In ancient Greek the technical term for an independent state was *polis*. Geographically a *polis* covered a very small area, usually much less than a modern county. This was often, but not always, separated from its neighbors by sea or hills. Athens, with 1000 square miles, was one of the largest Greek states; offshore lay a little island, 6 by 10 miles, Ceos, which was divided into four states!

Within the area of a *polis* all citizens assembled periodically at a focal point. In early days this center had been no more than a fortress in time of war (like the Acropolis) or a group of villages; but in historic times it was a small city in the economically more advanced areas. At the center the citizens worshipped the patron deity of the *polis* (Athena at Athens, for example), engaged in trade and judicial argument, and carried on virtually all of their political activity even though they might live in villages dotted about the landscape of the *polis*.

In treaties and histories, however, the abstract name of a *polis* has no place. It is "the Athenians" or "the Corinthians" who make laws, issue money, and take other sovereign actions. The citizens of a *polis* felt themselves tightly bound together and separated from the citizens of any other state. As a result a Greek *polis* could not easily expand its territory or admit resident foreigners to citizenship; but its jealous local pride made it ready to fight with its neighbors for the slightest causes. In the course of Greek history, wars were as frequent as they have been in modern European history. These tight social and political units jelled out of a much more fluid tribal society just a little before 700 B.C., and the wave of colonization about that time had spread the *polis* form widely over Mediterranean shores.

The citizens of a *polis* had duties and rights, the latter of which were often written down in codes of law. The major internal problem in any state was that which has caused trouble in many modern countries: just who is considered politically capable of running the country? Often this problem led in Greece to violent disagreements and civil wars in which there were ruthless killings.

In the 7th century B.C., or even earlier, most states got rid of their inherited kings in favor of the emerging aristocracies; but as trade and industry grew there appeared self-made men who also felt they had a political place. By 500, accordingly, most but not all Greek states had had to shift to an "oligarchic" pattern, in which political activity depended not on birth (as in aristocracies) but on wealth.

The Political Development of Athens 🖾🖾🖾🖾🖾🖾🖾🖾🖾🖾🖾🖾🖾🖾🖾

The *polis* of Athens was somewhat unusual in its early development. In the 7th century it too had been dominated by aristocrats, who oppressed the poorer farmers and even sold them into slavery if they could not repay their loans of wheat; after great unrest the reformer Solon was elected "reconciler" in 594.

Solon had already written a good deal of poetry (prose not yet being known) which expressed a high political and ethical spirit. If there was injustice anywhere in the state, Solon argued, it directly or indirectly affected everyone, even though he went inside his house and locked the door. Solon is the first person in Greek history of whom we know enough to visualize as an individual human being. He was a man who so deeply enjoyed life that he was willing to grow old, unlike his fellow Greeks; always he preached moderation and insisted that virtue was not a product just of being rich. For later Athenians he became a model much as George Washington became for Americans.

During his term of office in 594 Solon dealt firmly with the most pressing problem. He abolished enslavement of Athenian citizens because of debt and redeemed all the Athenian slaves he could. Then he divided the citizens into four classes on the basis of wealth. Only the three upper classes could hold public office, but all citizens could attend the Assembly or serve in the courts of law. Although this was not yet democracy, every citizen had some voice. In addition he rewrote the law code of the state, reducing the severe penalties in the earlier code (ascribed to a man called Draco), and encouraged the growth of industries. From Solon's time on, Athenian black-figured pottery and olive oil became staple items of export through which Athens could pay for foreign wheat to feed its ever-growing urban center.

After his reforms Solon left Athens for 10 years. A famous story told by Herodotus and others is that on his travels Solon visited King Croesus of Lydia. After Croesus had shown his visitor his wealth, he asked Solon, "Who is the happiest man you have ever seen?" The king was very surprised when Solon named Tellus, the

Athenian, who "had been an honest man, had had good children, an adequate estate, and died bravely in battle for his country." The story is false, for Croesus lived a generation after Solon. The Greeks told it to point up the difference between the true Greek citizen and a Near Eastern despot and to illustrate their traditional view that no man could be counted happy until the end of his life was known.

Solon had not dealt as adequately with the political problems of Athens as with its economic difficulties. Aristocratic groups continued their contests for control of public positions. Eventually a shrewd aristocrat called Pisistratus managed to gain control of Athens by force in 546. A man who rose to power illegally and kept his control by force was called a "tyrant" in Greek history; there were many tyrants in various parts of Greece, but Pisistratus was one of the most successful. After his death in 527, his sons Hippias and Hipparchus inherited his power and ruled Athens down to 510.

Although his power rested on his bodyguard, Pisistratus outwardly maintained the legal forms of government, like a city boss of today. Once when he was summoned as defendant on a charge of murder he politely came and was ready to defend himself, but his accuser did not have the nerve to appear. More important, Pisistratus and his sons encouraged the ownership of land in small farms, promoted foreign trade, and encouraged industrialists. In the last decades of the 6th century, Athenian potters changed from the style of pottery in which the figures were black and the background red (black-figured style) to a new technique in which the figures were red against a black background (red-figured style). Also the state began to issue the type of coins known as Attic "owls." These continued to be struck in much the same pattern for 300 years.

The tyrants beautified the city which had been developing in a hodge-podge fashion below the Acropolis and encouraged patriotism by elaborating great religious festivals for Athena. Abroad, however, they sought to remain peaceful although they did gain control of the Hellespont, which was the great artery for trade with the grain-growing regions of south Russia and the Black Sea fisheries. In 514 Hipparchus was murdered by two Athenian aristocrats, Harmodius and Aristogeiton, celebrated in later days in song and statues as "the tyrant slayers." Hippias then became more ruthless and was finally forced out of Athens in 510 by a combined effort of discontented Athenians and a Spartan expedition. The Spartans, the major military power in Greece by this date, disliked tyrants in general.

Time Chart No. 1: Athens 600-431 B.C.

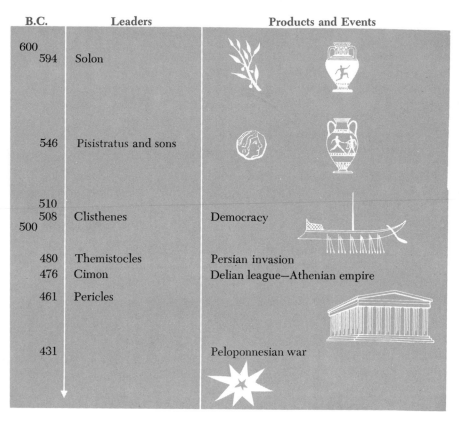

B.C.	Leaders	Products and Events
600 594	Solon	
546	Pisistratus and sons	
510 508 500	Clisthenes	Democracy
480	Themistocles	Persian invasion
476	Cimon	Delian league—Athenian empire
461	Pericles	
431		Peloponnesian war

After the expulsion of Hippias the Athenians were split between a conservative leader and a liberal leader. Clisthenes, the liberal, finally gained the upper hand in 508, largely because he appealed to the common citizens. In consequence he reorganized the government of the *polis* so that full power lay in the citizen Assembly.

From this point on, Athens was essentially a democracy or "rule of the people," though Clisthenes called it a system of "equal rights" (*isonomia*); the word "democracy" itself did not come into general use until the 5th century. Subsequent leaders of the Athenian people helped it to repel the Persians in 480 and finally to gain control over the Aegean, as we shall see later; by 440 the Athenian citizens were more deeply attached to democracy than those in any other *polis*.

3

The Golden Age
of Athenian Democracy

The Athenian Democracy in 440 回回回回回回回回回回回回回回回回回回回回回回回回回
The voice of Cleon and his fellow citizens was the source of constitutional power in the Athenian democracy. Ideas were expressed
directly in the Assembly, which consisted of all male citizens over
18 years of age who were willing to attend the sessions held about
every 10 days. There was no system of representatives as in modern
democracies. A rural citizen who wanted to vote had to trudge in
from the country the night before a major meeting in order to get
up at daybreak and be present in person on the rocky hillside of the
Pnyx; to encourage attendance the state police swept the Agora
clean of loafing citizens just before the meetings. Anyone who could
make himself heard by the 6000 and more voters who attended the
Assembly could speak on an issue, but clearly only those leaders
who commanded the respect of the voters would be listened to. In
this "direct" democracy, whatever the people decided at the Assembly was the law.

We might think that such a system would lead to anarchy or at
least would produce arbitrary decisions and unstable policies as the
will of the people fluctuated. These were real dangers, as the history
of Athens occasionally demonstrated; but they are dangers of modern democracies as well.

On the whole Athenian democracy did work. The primary reason

The meeting place of the Assembly was the rocky hillside of the Pnyx, a hill west of the Acropolis. Anyone who could gain the attention of the citizens from the speaker's platform, shown here, could speak. Demosthenes, the most famous Greek orator, is said to have cured himself of stuttering by practicing with a mouthful of pebbles; but to prepare himself for the ordeal of speaking here he yelled on the seashore against the noise of the breaking waves.

for this success was, as in any system, the quality of the citizens. From the days of Solon the Athenians had a tradition of avoiding extremes and of sober devotion to the common good. The problems on which they had to vote, moreover, were far simpler than those of a modern democracy, and in the Agora most citizens could pick up the necessary information by which to judge these problems. Not all Athenians, it must be remembered, were interested in politics or went to the Assembly; but those who did knew more about their system of government than do most citizens of modern democracies.

In addition, constitutional safeguards were built into the system. Any law passed by the Assembly had to be proposed by some one

Alison Frantz

The upper pot fragment has "Themistocles (son of) Neocles" on it; the lower one gives his name as it would have appeared on citizen registers, "Themistocles (of the deme) Phrearroi." The date when these were used in an ostracism was perhaps 483 or about 470 (when Themistocles actually was exiled). Hundreds of *ostraca* have been found where they were dumped to fill up holes in the Agora; one voter against Themistocles was angry enough to add, "Out with him!"

person, whose name was set forth at its beginning (see the example illustrated on page 200). If the citizens later thought they had made a mistake in passing it, they could attack the law in a court on a "writ of unconstitutionality," that is, as being contrary to Athenian principles. If the law were thus challenged within a year after its passage and found unconstitutional, its proposer was fined a sum that would bankrupt almost any citizen.

Another protection which was useful for a while against unwise or too ambitious politicians was the unpopularity contest called "ostracism." If the Assembly decided to carry out an ostracism vote in any year, a special date was set at which citizens wrote on clay sherds (*ostraca*) the name of the man they most disliked. Anyone who got a majority (if more than 6000 votes had been cast) was sent into exile for 10 years.

The most important step which allowed the Assembly to function in some order was Clisthenes' institution of a steering committee, the Council of 500. The shrewd Clisthenes redivided the Athenian citizenry into 10 new electoral districts, called "tribes," each of which consisted of precincts from the city proper, the coastal district, and the inland areas. In the rural part these precincts were the old villages or "demes," which had some limited self-government. Each precinct named candidates over 30 years of age for the Council of 500; from these candidates 50 were chosen *by lot* for each tribe to serve as members of the Council of 500 for a year. The final choice by lot was one of the most democratic steps imaginable and reduced the dangers of political skulduggery, but Clisthenes went even further to reduce the threat that the Council itself could turn into an inner government: members served only one year; no man could be a member two years in a row; and no one could serve more than twice in his lifetime.

The Council of 500 prepared the published agenda for each session of the Assembly. According to regular rules the Assembly would take up no issue not already investigated by the Council; normally the Council made a recommendation to the Assembly as to the best solution of each problem. The Council was divided into 10 subcommittees (the 50 members from each tribe forming 1 subcommittee); when its turn came, a subcommittee had to meet every day and eat lunch in the Tholos on the west side of the Agora so as to watch the government for its tenth of the year. In turn about one-third of this subcommittee had always to be on hand in the council chamber night and day in case an emergency arose, and it provided a chairman if the Assembly met.

Once the Assembly had passed a resolution, the executive branch carried it out on behalf of the people and the Council of 500 supervised the execution. Almost all of the administrative officials were chosen by lot for one year. Usually they were selected in groups of 10 to carry out one specific function such as policing the markets or caring for the streets; the street commissioners had a body of public slaves specifically to pick up the bodies of people who died at night in the streets, and public slaves did other work for the community. All officials chosen by lot were examined by the Council before

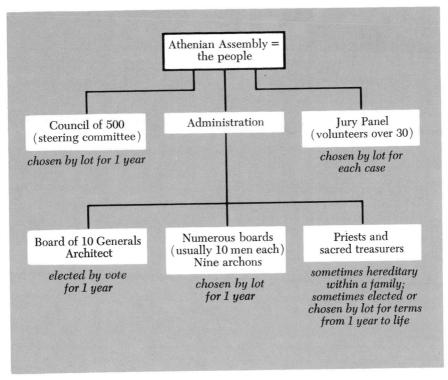

entering office to eliminate the physically or mentally incompetent; and any official handling public monies was subject to repeated inspections. The Athenians had great faith in democracy in theory but had little trust in the incorruptibility of any one individual.

Where did leadership come from, if public officers were chosen by lot? In earlier centuries the main executive officials had been the nine archons, who had been elected by the aristocracy to be leaders. One of these, the "archon eponymos," gave his name to the year he served in (the year of Themistocles thus was what we call 493 B.C.); another, the "king archon," had supervised religious functions which the earlier kings had carried out; a third was "war leader," and the other six were "law-keepers," in charge of justice. From 487 on, however, the archons also were chosen by lot from a group of 500 candidates selected by the demes, thus limiting their power to lead the community. After serving their year the archons became permanent members of an advisory council called the council of the Areopagus, but after 462 the powers of this body too were restricted and confined to religious rites.

The only officials who were actually elected by public vote were the city architect, obviously needing special talent, and also the Board of 10 Generals; for Cleon and his fellow citizens did not feel like entrusting their lives in war to officials chosen by lot. The result was that the Board of 10 Generals became the real leaders of the people in the 5th century. In 440, as for many years, Pericles was the major figure on this board. We shall examine his power in a moment.

One part of the government remains to be considered: the courts of law, which were really committees of the people. Each year a panel of 6000 jurors over 30 years of age was drawn up from those who volunteered to serve. For each trial a jury of 201 or more was drawn by a very complicated system of lots so that bribery and influence could be limited. Each of the two parties in a lawsuit had to speak and act for himself, though he could hire a professional speechwriter to compose his speech. Undoubtedly, one had to be very careful as to how one appealed to the elders of the community who sat on the jury and determined by majority vote their verdict. There could be no appeal from this committee of the people in its judicial capacity; in verdicts of capital punishment one was sometimes allowed to commit suicide by drinking poison, except those who were found guilty of murder and the like. These unfortunate culprits were attached to a vertical plank on which they hung until they died.

Pericles

Democracies succeed only if the people are willing to choose and to support able leaders, and Athenian democracy had permanently given its support to the mighty Pericles. Born of the same aristocratic family as Clisthenes two generations earlier, Pericles so dominated the later 5th century that it is sometimes called the Periclean Age.

Pericles rose by helping to curtail the powers of the conservative council of the Areopagus. About 451 he introduced state pay for service on the Council of 500 or as jurors; thus, even poor citizens could take part in public life. Another popular law which he supported limited Athenian citizenship to children both of whose parents were Athenians; citizenship was now a privilege at Athens. Ironically enough, his own son was born of a woman from Miletus and later had to be given citizenship specially.

Throughout the 440's and 430's Pericles was elected year after year to the Board of 10 Generals, and normally he could persuade the Assembly to support his policies of democracy at home and imperialism abroad. Along with his own personal ambition and his patriotic desire to see Athens great, Pericles also had lofty ideals for uplifting his fellow citizens culturally and spent public money lavishly to beautify Athens. As he put it, these public works gave employment to the citizens, and the result was the embellishment of the Acropolis with the great buildings which have made it famous ever since.

Despite his democratic program Pericles did not mix with common citizens in his personal life, which remained private and simple.

Fototeca Unione

According to a writer of comedies Pericles' skull was misshapen and so he preferred to be shown with a helmet on his head. This is a Roman copy (in the Vatican); the lettering reads, "Pericles (son of) Xanthippus, Athenian."

His friends were philosophers, artists, and musicians. Nonetheless his name is indissolubly connected with one of the world's great democracies; ancient writers and modern historians alike tend to idealize him. Pericles was incorruptible—a rare quality among Athenian politicians—a masterful speaker, and a clear thinker. Reason and emotion lived together in his breast in remarkable harmony, for he was fired by a great vision of the perfectibility of man in general and of the political greatness of Athens in particular.

This vision has perhaps led later students of his career to disregard some deep defects in his political programs. To judge a public leader is never easy, but certainly Pericles' popularity gave little room for other politicians; after his death no one of his caliber came forward as popular leader. He encouraged the democracy to be uncompromising. Worst of all, he ruthlessly pushed Athenian imperialism and directly led Athens into the great Peloponnesian war with Sparta (431–404), which in the end ruined his own country.

Yet Pericles must also be given credit for his noble aspirations; some of these appear in his Funeral Oration, which is quoted in Part III. Only so long as the Athenian citizens supported him could Pericles remain powerful; that they accepted his severe leadership is perhaps the greatest mark of the quality of their democracy.

Debate on Democracy
Nowadays most men in the Western world think—or say in public that they think—democracy is the best form of government. So they tend to look back favorably on the first great democracy in Western civilization. Others, however, can see serious defects in Athenian democracy. Actually the good and bad sides of this form of government have been the subject of excited debate ever since it came into existence in the 5th century B.C., and most of the criticisms which are made of modern democracy were already being voiced then.

Many aristocrats simply did not believe that most men had the ability to pass political judgments; was Cleon's vote entitled to have the same weight as that of an educated, wealthy man? They were horrified too by the freedom of speech at Athens, which permitted the comic poets to make scurrilous attacks on public figures. Others assailed democracy more insidiously by pointing out its weaknesses in practice. Pericles was accused of being a democratic tyrant who gained general favor for himself by spending public funds on the populace. The Assembly was called fickle and bloodthirsty; during the Peloponnesian war Aristophanes leveled barbed shafts at the willingness of the people to follow leaders who promised rewards, played on superstitions, and otherwise appealed to baser instincts in order to gain power. The great historian Thucydides placed the blame for the Athenian collapse in this war squarely on the shoulders of the people for judging foreign policy incorrectly, though, as he indicates, the citizens tried to blame their leaders for their own poor decisions.

Nowadays the same criticisms recur; but radical democrats attack the Athenian system from the other side as having been not democratic enough. For Athens did not allow foreigners, slaves, and women to vote, and of some 45,000 male citizens, not more than 6000 or so usually attended the Assembly. In judging these criticisms, however, an American citizen today might ask himself, Who could vote in the United States in the days of Thomas Jefferson? or What percentage of the potential voters in my home district normally vote in a minor election?

Despite the undeniable occasional defects of democratic practice, the Athenians clung to their way of government in prosperity and defeat alike, with the exception of one brief lapse just after the Peloponnesian war. Athens was a democracy from 508 to 267 B.C., the longest-lived democracy which has yet existed. No democratic structure, moreover, has gone further, by direct vote and the use of the lot, to ensure that every citizen had the same power. If Cleon took his political rights seriously, he would have spent about two years of his life serving on the Council of 500 or in one of the many administrative jobs, as well as attending the Assembly up to 40 times a year.

The Athenian Empire
The evolution of democracy at home was intimately connected with the increasing imperialism of Athens abroad. The commercial and industrial elements, which benefited from the growth of seaborne trade, were a bulwark of the Assembly. In turn, the general unity of all classes made it possible for Athens to exert greater strength abroad. The result was a sea-based empire spread over much of the Aegean.

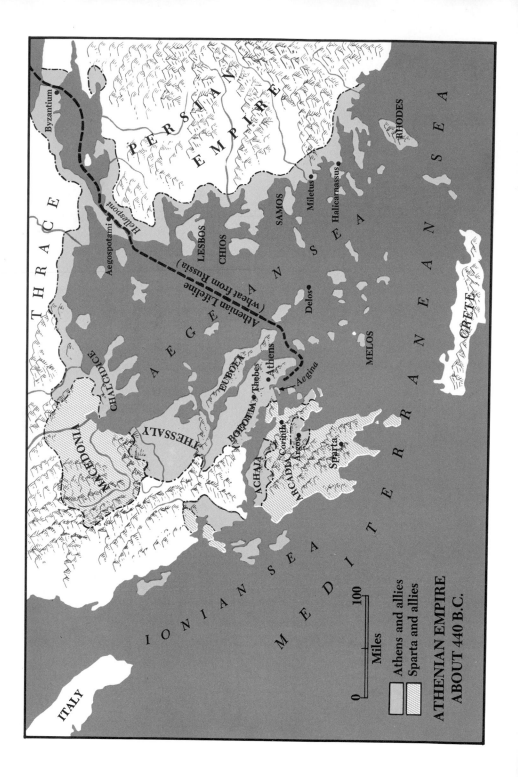

THE RISE OF GREEK CIVILIZATION

ATHENIAN EMPIRE
ABOUT 440 B.C.

Athens and allies
Sparta and allies

Miles
0   100

This empire had begun 40 years earlier as a voluntary association of Greek states, the Delian league, which wanted to keep back the Persians after their invasion of Greece in 480–479 B.C. Athens was by far the largest member of this league and more or less unconsciously converted the voluntary into an involuntary bond over the next three decades.

At its height the Athenian empire covered some 170 Greek communities on the north and east coasts of the Aegean, reaching from Byzantium down to the south coast of Asia Minor. The empire had a population of some 2 million people; but Athenian naval power was an important factor all the way from Sicily to the Black Sea. Almost all subject states paid an annual tribute totaling about 400 talents a year (1 talent had 6000 drachmas, and a drachma was more than a day's pay for a worker). Much of this money was spent as soon as it came in; the surplus was stored on the Acropolis at Athens.

The dependent states also had to follow Athenian foreign policy; use Athenian weights, measures, and coins; and send major lawsuits to Athens, which thus could protect its local friends. Generally the subjects could have any form of government they wished, even tyranny so long as it was loyal; but if they revolted, Athens was likely to favor institution of a democracy on reconquest. Loyalty to the imperial master was also encouraged by the presence of Athenian colonies or garrisons at certain points and by a variety of traveling inspectors; ultimately obedience was forced by the Athenian navy, the costs of which were paid by the tribute of the subjects. In peacetime some 60 triremes, each with a crew of 200 men (150 rowers and others), would be at sea for eight months of the year.

Just as the Athenians created the first great democracy, so too they developed the first important empire in Western civilization. They argued about building an empire far more openly and fiercely than have subsequent imperialists (who sometimes have not been aware they *were* imperialists). Athenian subjects, however, had only limited opportunity to enter the debate; if they expressed any disagreements by revolts or failure to pay tribute, they were treated ruthlessly by Athens. Many subjects felt that their position was one of "slavery," but traders appreciated the security of the seas brought by the Athenian navy and also the prosperity of the period.

Many Athenians, however, were troubled. They felt uneasy at the free manner in which Pericles used the tribute of the empire to beautify Athens itself; the subjection of fellow Greeks seemed unjust;

4 drachma   1 drachma   obol

These are typical Athenian silver coins of the 5th century (6 obols = 1 drachma). Some other large denominations were struck occasionally; but even the 4-drachma coin, which weighs about 17 grams, represented more than a week's pay for a skilled workman. More important to Cleon would be the little coins (half-obols were also struck); when a man went to the Agora he tucked one or two small coins in his mouth. Greek clothes had no pockets.

On the obverse is the head of Athena, the goddess who protected the state. She is shown with a helmet; after the defeat of the Persians the helmet was decorated with olive leaves. On the reverse is her owl. To its upper left on the 4-drachma piece are an olive sprig and a crescent moon; to the right are the three first letters of "Athenian."

When the Athenians used the treasury of their empire to beautify the Acropolis or for purposes of war they coined millions of the 4-drachma pieces. Since Athenian silver was very pure and reliable, it came to be used in trade all over the Mediterranean.

"Owls" have been found in hoards as far as Afghanistan, and the type was widely imitated by local coinages in the Near East. Along with the modern American dollar bill and the English gold sovereign the Athenian 4-drachma coin is one of the great forms of currency in history.

conservative landowners did not like the way the naval empire encouraged the trading and industrial lower classes. In an ostracism contest in 443, the anti-imperialists tried to get rid of Pericles; but the result was that their leader was ostracized. Cleon and his friends were too proud of Athenian power and wealth to give up foreign rule. Even the Parthenon was a product of imperialism: tributes had paid its costs.

Later the historian Thucydides drew a grim picture of how the Athenians equated might and right, grew increasingly vindictive in killing rebels, and dreamed of ruling all the Greek world (see Part III). Democracy at home made imperialism abroad more inevitable and ruthless, and Athenian imperialism in time led to the mighty fall of Athens in 404; for the free Greeks who lived in Sparta, Corinth, and elsewhere eventually became deeply alarmed by Athenian expansion. But no one in the period of Periclean prosperity could foresee the future.

There is, however, another view of the picture to be kept in mind, for imperialism is not necessarily as bad an institution as it is often depicted to be. As long as Athens was master of the Aegean, its merchants were free from the danger of piracy, and the Greek world as a whole was safe from Persia. After the fall of Athens, as we shall see later, Persia became more and more the ultimate judge of what happened in 4th-century Greece.

The School of Greece
In his Funeral Oration, Pericles calls Athens "the school of Greece," and certainly in the time of Pericles, Athens became the center to which foreign thinkers were drawn, as they now may be drawn to London or New York. In the same period, native-born Athenians were writing those tragedies and comedies which are the first great achievements of Western drama, and other men were turning the Acropolis into an eternal home of beauty. This artistic and literary outburst is one of the most concentrated and amazing triumphs of all human history.

Why did it take place? At any one time most men live from day to day, earning their daily bread and enduring the cares and uncertainties of human existence; if Cleon went beyond these chores, he could spend most of his time on his duties as a citizen and a ruler of a large empire. Still, all phases of life were tightly interwoven in this small, closely knit country. Artistic and literary developments, then, were not entirely separate matters for experts, but were directly tied to the religious and public life of Athens. The revenues of the empire and of Athens' growing commerce provided surplus money; the confidence and expansiveness of the age encouraged men to create boldly; most important of all, Greek civilization had developed a solid basis for great achievements.

Temples which are masterpieces of refinement and harmony were erected in the 5th century all over the Greek world (see page 131). Sculptors too were busy everywhere; probably the greatest sculptural decoration of any temple is that of the Temple of Zeus at Olympia. Of the poets of this age the greatest was Pindar of Thebes, who celebrated the aristocratic merits of victors at the great athletic games in shimmering, virtually untranslatable Greek verse. Nowhere, however, was there such an outpouring as at Athens.

Higher Learning 𐄂𐄂𐄂𐄂𐄂𐄂𐄂𐄂𐄂𐄂𐄂𐄂𐄂𐄂𐄂𐄂𐄂𐄂𐄂𐄂𐄂𐄂𐄂𐄂𐄂𐄂𐄂𐄂𐄂𐄂𐄂𐄂
Later we shall walk about Athens to see the buildings which were being erected during the lifetime of Cleon; here let us look at the parallel activities in literature. Down to the 5th century virtually all Greek writing was in the form of poetry, but shortly before 500, prose had been developed as a literary means of expression. Sometimes it was used for scholarly work, including the medical treatises which go under the name of Hippocrates. (We do not, incidentally, know very much that is certain about this great doctor; but it is clear that Greek medicine, unlike earlier semi-religious superstitions, assigned earthly causes to human illnesses and sought to cure them by rational means for the first time.) Other prose work of the 5th century included the great histories of Herodotus and Thucydides, philosophical essays, and orations.

The busy, practical Athenians of this period were not much interested in knowledge for its own sake. The philosopher-scientist Anaxagoras, the first to know the real causes of eclipses, came to Athens and discussed his theories about the origins of the world; but when he asserted the sun, usually considered a god, was really a molten rock larger than the Peloponnesus the Athenians expelled him for irreligious thoughts. Soon after 440, however, Athens began to draw from all over the Greek world teachers called "sophists," men who could impart the useful skills of oratory and argument; these sophists were the real founders of advanced education and began the formal study of rhetoric, logic, and grammar. At the same time they were sharp critics of ancestral political and religious conventions.

Tragedy and Comedy ㈲㈲㈲㈲㈲㈲㈲㈲㈲㈲㈲㈲㈲㈲㈲㈲㈲㈲㈲
The greatest Athenian contribution to literature was the rise of drama. Twice a year, tragedies and comedies were performed at festivals in honor of the god Dionysus. The details of how they were produced are described later (see page 75), but here we will consider some of the greatest playwrights.

Of the comedies, only some of the works of Aristophanes have been preserved. These are remarkably varied in subject. One play, the *Clouds,* is a bitter attack on the philosopher Socrates, who is portrayed as a sophist leading the young to make fun of their elders. Another comedy, the *Frogs,* assaults the tragedian Euripides as also corrupting the younger generation; here Aristophanes expects his audience to be able to appreciate mock quotations from Aeschylus and Euripides. The *Birds* is a marvelous fantasy of some Athenians, discontented with the lawsuits and contentions of their daily life, who try to live with the birds and set up an ideal Birdland. Others are direct attacks on major political leaders or on the war with Sparta then raging. Whatever their subject, these comedies combine lyric poetry, quick repartee, and outright obscenity in a frankness of speech rarely equaled in later ages.

The subject of a tragedy was usually a legend of the heroic age, such as the war of Argos and Thebes or the tales clustered about the Homeric heroes; but plays might also deal with historic events. The one surviving example of the latter type is Aeschylus' *Persians,* performed in 472 with Pericles as producer.

Narration of a story or legend, however, was only a means by which the author might explore the nature of mankind; and in doing so, the tragedian turned firmly away from realistic depictions of Athenian citizens to an ideal level of heroic men and women. Even the gods themselves might appear on occasion. However great, the human beings in a tragedy had flaws which led them to ruin; the authors who brought these heroes to life before Cleon and his fellow citizens sought not so much to explain how the universe operated as to illuminate the greatnesses and defects of mankind.

Although many authors vied in the annual competitions, the three who were considered the greatest were Aeschylus, Sophocles, and Euripides. Aeschylus was a deeply religious thinker, although at times he exhibits the strong hold of earlier tradition. His plays, like the *Agamemnon,* are brooding dramas of inevitable, catastrophic ruin, in which passion is still ill-restrained and in which the religious and aristocratic qualities of 6th-century Greece are powerful. His characters stand almost outside the human world, and his poetry rumbles with the thunder of bold images.

Most balanced and serene of the three was Sophocles, who was a friend of Pericles and on occasion an elected general of the Athenian democracy. He is said to have written 123 plays and won first place 24 times, but only 7 plays are preserved. The greatest of these is generally considered to be *Oedipus the King,* performed shortly after 430.

Oedipus, son of King Laius and Queen Jocasta of Thebes, was born under a prophecy that he would kill his father and marry his mother; left to die on a rocky hillside as a result, he was saved by a shepherd and grew up in Corinth ignorant of his parentage. Near Delphi he did unwittingly murder his father and then went to Thebes, where he married and had children by his own mother.

The play itself opens at the point where a plague has descended on Thebes, and Oedipus, as defender of his subjects, promises to rescue them. When a messenger from Delphi reveals that the god Apollo has ordered Thebes to punish the murderer of Laius, Oedipus fiercely calls down curses on the culprit. The audience, which knew the truth, must have shuddered at his self-confident anger.

Step by step Oedipus draws closer to the truth. The blind seer Tiresias is goaded by the king into hinting at the actual facts, which Oedipus does not comprehend. Thereafter a messenger from Corinth and the shepherd of Laius' house, who once had taken the babe to the hills, reveal all. Jocasta, a rationalist who disdains the seers, first detects the truth, rushes into the palace, and kills herself. When Oedipus realizes that he has actually fulfilled the prophecy, he rushes off to blind himself. At the end only the chorus remains on the stage, to point the moral:

> You that live in my ancestral Thebes, behold this Oedipus,—him who knew the famous riddles and was a man most masterful; not a citizen who did not look with envy on his lot—see him now and see the breakers of misfortune swallow him! Look upon that last day always. Count

no mortal happy till he has passed the final limit of his life secure from pain.*

With Euripides, the last of the three great tragedians, we step almost outside the boundaries of 5th-century civilization. In his lifetime Euripides was rarely successful, for he won first prize only five times. Before his death he had abandoned the tottering, bitter Athens of the Peloponnesian war and withdrew to Macedonia, where he wrote the *Bacchae* and some other plays. Yet his skepticism about the divine government of the world and his sympathetic treatment of human passion in such female figures as Medea, Alcestis, and Iphigenia made him a favorite of later ages; no ancient playwright appears more often on the modern stage than Euripides.

The Nature of Man

The 5th-century view of man is nowhere better displayed than in the Attic tragedies. Again and again a great man or woman stepped forth upon the stage, only to be stripped of pride and often to die violently in ruin. The vehicle for the ruin was a man's own flaws, for man was free; and yet behind all lay the immortal gods, who punished undue pride (*hybris*). In tragedy the moral lesson was to cultivate *sophrosyne*, a proper balance and awareness of one's true position.

Nonetheless the tragedians shared a pride in man's achievements and his independence of action. Most noble of all is the great praise by the chorus in Sophocles' *Antigone*, which begins, "Wonders are many, and none is more wonderful than man." Man crosses the sea, harnesses the earth, teaches himself word-swift thought and speech; "cunning beyond fancy's dream is the fertile skill which brings him, now to evil, now to good."

The balanced view of man; the serene, even severe temper of tragedy; the welling passion which is restrained almost unconsciously by a sense of proper form—all these are qualities of what we call the "Classic outlook." In a play such as *Oedipus the King* the tempo is slow and deliberate at the outset, but speeds up irresistibly; the reflective chorus which gives occasional relief in its lyric odes, the hot-

---

* Translated by David Grene. The concluding view, count no man happy until he is dead, was a famous one in Greek thought, as we saw in the story of Solon and Croesus.

headed Oedipus, his wife and mother Jocasta—calm and consoling at first, then, increasingly horrified—and all the other characters are pitted against each other in subtle rhythms. Like Classic art and architecture the play has an outwardly simple, austere treatment which omits the insignificant diversions, on-stage violence, and by-plots so evident in Shakespeare's plays. The whole development of *Oedipus the King* takes only 1530 lines. Yet the tight logical construction of the play, its skillful proportions, and its artistic quality are a superb example of the developed Greek mind. When Oedipus fiercely proclaimed, "I must not hear of not discovering the whole truth," he expressed the consistent effort of the Greek thinker to plunge to the heart of a problem, no matter what the cost.

The Citizens of Athens. Cleon and his fellow men and women of Athens in 440 B.C. were surely harassed often by the grinding cares of daily life, and not all of them liked the changes which were brought by democracy at home and imperialism abroad, or the criticism of ancestral ways voiced by the more advanced and liberated thinkers. Most of this criticism, however, was yet to come after Athens fell into a long, exhausting war with Sparta which ended its empire.

In the great days of Periclean Athens its citizens were still optimistic and enthusiastic as they met to gossip in the Agora, to vote in the Assembly, or to pour out to the festivals of Dionysus, where they cheered at comic thrusts or shivered at the fall of a mighty hero. Both politically and intellectually the achievements of this small community over two generations are a mighty illumination of the nature and possibilities of mankind, a marvelous illustration of what the chorus of the *Antigone* meant. Those achievements have been an inspiration and model for men ever since.

**Art and
Architecture in
the Periclean Age**

**The Production
of an
Athenian Play**

**The Rediscovery
of Early
Greek History**

ART AND ARCHITECTURE IN
THE PERICLEAN AGE

In the generation before Pericles the city of Athens, including its Acropolis, had been destroyed in the great Persian invasion of 480–479 B.C. To the men and women of that time the blow must have seemed a complete catastrophe. Actually it left the way open for a tremendous rebuilding of Athens once the state was again strong and rich enough to do so.

Immediately after the invasion the Athenians had devoted their limited energies to building a wall around the city and also around the harbor of Piraeus, in which they re-used old tombstones and other already prepared stones (one of these is shown on page 36). Then in the time of Pericles (459 on) they built the famous Long Walls, about four miles long, which connected the city and the harbor; Athens itself was virtually an island on land, for without gunpowder it was very difficult for an attacking army to break down a defended wall. The rest of the Athenian energies went into public buildings; individual houses, as we have seen, were scarcely more than plastered hovels.

Over the countryside of Athens a number of temples and theaters were built. Cape Sunium is still crowned by the lonely, half-ruined temple of Poseidon, the first landmark of Athens one sees when coming in by ship or plane from Asia and Africa. Most of the new buildings, however, were concentrated in the Agora and on the nearby Acropolis of Athens itself.

In the Agora the first public structure to be restored was the Tholos, the meeting place of the Council of 500. Not until about 462 did the Athenians proceed much further in reorganizing their marketplace. Then they built the Painted Porch (*Stoa*), a long colonnade adorned by paintings of the legendary sack of Troy and the historical battle of Marathon. Aristotle later placed their painter, Polygnotus, beside the tragedian Sophocles as "showing men better than they are" and in revealing qualities of character; but these great works, like all other major Greek paintings, have long since disappeared. Then came altars and temples to many gods. The greatest still standing, and the most perfect temple left in Athens, is the temple of Hephaestus (sometimes called the Theseum) on a little knoll overlooking the Agora proper. The only statues of human beings in the Agora were those of the "tyrant slayers," Harmodius and Aristogeiton, new works which replaced the earlier set looted by the Persians.

Three hundred feet above the Agora and the simple homes of the Athenian citizens towered the rock of the Acropolis, the earthly home of Athena and the other divine protectors of the state. Its north wall, facing the Agora, was put together out of stones that were left after the Persian destruction; the southern wall, of more regular stonework, came in the 460's. Not until 448 did Athens, at the prompting of Pericles, begin to pour imperial revenues into the decoration of this small hilltop, less than 300 by 200 yards in size.

As a modern tourist approaches the Acropolis by a steep path, he comes first to the magnificent Doric entry gate (the Propylaea), which was left unfinished because of the Peloponnesian war. On a spur running out to the right is a little jewel, the delicately finished Ionic temple of Athena Nike (Bringer of Victory).* Inside the Propylaea the top of the limestone hill was once covered by a host of inscribed stones, altars, and dedications of works of art and of trophies. Almost all of these have disappeared across the subsequent centuries, but two temples still survive.

At the very crest stands the Parthenon, built 447–438 in honor of Athena the Virgin (Parthenos). Eventually it was remodeled into a Christian church, which protected it from destruction; but when the Turks took Greece it finally became a powder magazine. It exploded when it was hit in a Venetian attack on Athens in A.D. 1687. Today some of the damage has been repaired, and one can at least sense the amazing skill of its architect Ictinus.

* For diagrams of Doric and Ionic columns, see page 130.

The temple of Athena Nike had a sculptured balustrade. One panel, shown here, depicts Nike binding her sandal; in very shallow reliefs the sculptor has given the full sense of drapery and body with complete mastery.

The Acropolis, seen from the southwest. The tall hill behind, Lycabettus, played no part in Athenian history, but today one gets a marvelous panorama of all Athens and its plain from the top of Lycabettus.

The temple form, with its vertical columns and horizontal base and roofline, is essentially a box, intended to enclose the statue of the deity within; but over the previous 200 years the Greeks had refined and polished this simple architectural idea into a marvelous unity, the greatest example of which is the Parthenon. Architects had learned that from a distance, a straight line appears curved, and in compensation virtually every line of the Parthenon was skillfully curved so that it would look straight. The horizontal lines of the foundations and steps thus rise slightly from the ends to the middle. All the columns are subtly inclined inward and toward each other such that, if projected, their axes would meet at a point about 1½ miles above the building proper. Built out of marble which was brought over 11 miles from Mount Pentelicus and tugged up to the Acropolis, the Parthenon today has a golden hue as the iron in the marble has oxidized. All the stones

The Propylaea, or entry gate into the Acropolis.

were finished on the site with the most scrupulous and refined care. The Parthenon is marvelously harmonious; at the same time it is solid and severe and looks as if it had grown out of the rock.

Cooperating with Ictinus in the decoration of the Parthenon was Phidias, one of the greatest sculptors of the 5th century. Phidias designed the sculptures to fit in the triangular ends of the temple roof (pediments). On the east end these show the birth of Athena. The west end depicts the contest between Athena and Poseidon as to which deity would be master of Athens. (Athena won by giving the olive tree to Athens.) Around the outside of the Parthenon, above the columns, were inserted 92 rectangular metopes, scenes in legendary battles of the giants, Lapiths and Centaurs, and Amazons.

On the inside (*cella*) wall the Parthenon was unusual in having a long strip of sculpture, a frieze 172 yards long, which illustrated the march of the young men and women of Athens from the Dipylon Gate to the Acropolis to bring Athena a new *peplos* (robe) every four years during the festival called the Greater Panathenaea. Much of this frieze and the other majestic sculptures of the Parthenon were taken down early in the 19th century by Lord Elgin, British ambassador to Turkey, and transported to London, where they are now one of the greatest treasures in the British Museum.

Phidias also made the great statue of Athena placed inside the Parthenon, a standing figure over 30 feet high with Victory in her outstretched hand. Made primarily of gold plates attached to a wooden core, with flesh of ivory and eyes of precious stones, it is long since gone, but small replicas survive to suggest its appearance. Another statue by Phidias, of Athena Promachos (the Defender), was in bronze and stood outdoors; the tip of its shining spear could be seen by Athenian fleets entering the Piraeus harbor.

Across from the Parthenon stands the Erechtheum, a complicated temple on several levels built in 421–405 to counterbalance the Parthenon. Here the legendary hero Erechtheus was worshipped along with other ancestral figures; the most ancient statue of Athena, made of olive wood, was also enshrined in this temple. Coming out toward the Parthenon is the Maiden Porch, the roof of which is supported by 6 caryatids (female figures); beside them grew the sacred olive of Athena. On the other or Agora side the main porch of the Erechtheum has

The Parthenon, seen as one comes up from the Propylaea. The triangular space of the pediments is visible as also the rectangular spaces for the metopes; the frieze is high on the wall inside the columns. *Greek National Tourist Office*

The Erechtheum, seen as one comes up from the Propylaea; its many parts show clearly. The Maiden Porch has no entrance; it was intended only to help balance the building.

Ionic columns and an intricately decorated doorway. In Turkish times the Erechtheum was the harem of the governor of Athens, so the interior has suffered considerable remodeling and damage.

The buildings and statues of the Acropolis honored the gods and heroes who protected the Athenian state, but the magnificent ruins which still stand must remind any observer of those human beings, from the ordinary citizen Cleon to the leader Pericles, who in less than 50 years made this small site a lasting visible monument of the qualities of Greek civilization.

Above, a young Athenian aristocrat on horseback, from the frieze of the Parthenon. Below, water carriers in the sacred procession, from the same frieze. Although each figure is basically the same their poses are varied, and the figures are subtly linked to form an artistic composition.

THE PRODUCTION OF AN

ATHENIAN PLAY

Unlike modern plays, which are performed at schools and in commercial theaters, the tragedies and comedies of the 5th century were sponsored by the state and were presented at religious festivals in honor of the god Dionysus. Here they were given only once, though the more successful works might be performed again in later years.

The authors who wished to compete submitted their plays to the archon well before the festival. Each comedian offered one play; each of the tragedians had to prepare a set of three tragedies, which might or might not have a common theme, plus an afterpiece called a satyr play. The archon chose three to five comedies for each festival; in the field of tragedy he picked the best three sets and allotted to each tragedian his actors, paid at state expense, and a producer (called the *choregus*). The producer was necessarily a wealthy citizen, for he bore the expenses of the chorus, 12 to 15 men, and provided the costumes as his contribution to the glory of Dionysus.

On the appointed days for the festival the Athenian public trooped out to the theater of Dionysus, a structure with wooden seats on the south slope of the Acropolis, and paid their two obols apiece to the lessee who kept up the theater. Then they watched one play after another all morning. Judges drawn by lot awarded prizes. The poet who won got a crown of ivy; the *choregus*, the right to spend yet more money by setting up a triumphal tablet; the best actor, an inscription on a state list in the Agora.

This is a Roman mosaic showing on the left the mask of a female musician, and on the right the mask of a slave (often an important character in comedies in helping a son outwit his stubborn father).

The stage consisted of a circular orchestra with an altar of Dionysus, about which the chorus marched or solemnly danced, and a permanent backdrop representing a temple or palace. The actors proper performed on the shallow steps in front of the scenery or, if they depicted gods, might appear on an upper balcony.

In the earlier popular celebrations out of which the tragedies developed, the chorus had stood alone and sung. Even after actors had individual parts, the chorus still played a major role for a while, but then it shrank to the position of ideal spectator. In Aeschylus' plays it marched in, at the beginning, with a musician who played a type of double oboe (illustrated on page 127), and set the scene of the plot in an opening song; in the work of the other playwrights the chorus appeared later. Along the way the chorus voiced in lyric odes the thoughts

Hirmer Fotoarchiv München

Hundreds of theaters were built throughout the Greek world, usually on hillsides. While the theater at Athens is the most famous, the 4th-century theater at Epidaurus is better preserved and is used today for dramatic performances. Its acoustics are so good that anyone standing at the top, from which this picture is taken, can hear words spoken in the orchestra.

which the audience might have as it watched the tragedy unfold, and in Sophoclean tragedy it held the stage alone at the end of the play to reflect on the somber meaning of the scenes just witnessed.

A play might have any number of parts, but no more than three actors appeared on the stage at once. Since the actors wore masks, they could slip from one role to another easily; female parts were played by men. Some speeches were sung as odes; others were swift debates. An Athenian tragedy was in many ways like a modern opera, but we can judge it only as a play: the musical accompaniments have not survived.

THE REDISCOVERY OF EARLY GREEK HISTORY

Sooner or later a curious student of history will ask himself, "How does the historian know anything about the past? He can't see it." If we are writing about anything before our own lifetime, we can in truth rely only on evidence left to us by men of that period. This evidence we call "sources."

Can we trust a source simply because *it* is contemporary with the event? Obviously not; sources can be prejudiced or limited in their views. Being a historian is very close to being a detective, for one has to sniff out bias and dig below the surface of what a witness says.

Students of Greek history depend mainly on written records, which include poetry, inscribed stones, coins, and so on, as well as histories. Yet the alphabet came into use only in the 8th century B.C.; how do we know about the many centuries before that, which we are going to consider in the next chapter?

The rediscovery of this early Greek history is a fascinating tale in itself, involving romance, deceit and tricks, international rivalries, ruthless ambition, and always the drive of determined men to find out the truth. One hundred years ago historians could use only the Homeric epics, which were not intended to be genuine history, along with myths and legends. This type of evidence is colorful and full of exciting stories, but tales handed down orally across centuries do not have much historical value.

The Riches of Mycenae

When Schliemann found this gold face mask, which shows a bearded warrior, he telegraphed excitedly, "I have looked upon the face of Agamemnon." Actually the mask represents in its small, tight mouth, Grecian nose, and tuft of beard a much earlier warlord of Mycenae; four other masks were also found in the shaft graves.

Since then, however, archeologists have been busily digging up the Greek landscape, and it is on the results of their work that we now mainly rely. What they find is certainly contemporary evidence, but since it is not in written form we have to investigate very carefully just what the pots, tombs, and other physical material actually tell us about early Greece. The story in earlier pages could not have been told as recently as 50 years ago, and in another generation historians will tell much of it differently.

One of the most glamorous archeologists who have ever excavated was Heinrich Schliemann. Born in Germany in 1822, Schliemann had to go to work as a young boy. Somehow, he came upon a copy of Homer's *Iliad* and it fascinated him. When Schliemann found out that German scholars of the time doubted that Troy had ever existed, he decided to prove that his Homeric heroes had really lived. After spending some time in California during the Gold Rush, he made a fortune in Russia, trading in indigo and other commodities; eventually he became an American citizen in 1869, while delivering lectures at Indiana University.

By this time he had dug up a number of settlements, one atop another, at the hill which he called Troy; and in a very low level he found a rich treasure of gold vessels which he named the "Treasure of Priam." Scholars nowadays agree with Schliemann that this site was Troy, but feel that a much later layer than the one he picked corresponds to the legendary date of the Trojan wars.

Schliemann then moved to Greece, where the rock walls of Mycenae had always been visible along with the Treasury of Atreus. Here fortune smiled on his zeal again, for just inside the Lion Gate of the fortress he discovered a grave circle with 6 shafts cut down into the rock. These graves, which had never been disturbed, had 19 burials of Mycenaean princes, fully equipped with gold face masks, gold jewelry, ivory

The Lion Gate of Mycenae has always stood visible since its construction. The heads of the lions were made of separate pieces, which have been lost; the column, notice, has the typical Minoan taper downward.

Greek National Tourist Office

The Elegance of Cnossus

Photo by Harissiadis—Athens

From the central courtyard one descends this handsome staircase, built around a light well, to the Queen's Apartment overlooking the valley. Sir Arthur Evans restored much at Cnossus in concrete and painted it in the original colors.

Across the courtyard from the staircase is the throne room, with a simple gypsum throne and 2 "griffins" in a field of flowers—not the usual sort of decoration of a royal center. In the foreground is a sacred area, where the king may have been desperately appealing to his gods at the time when his palace was captured and burned. Evans found here a great oil jar, overturned, and religious utensils.

gaming boards, and other evidence of rich power which knew Cretan art. No single Aegean find has ever uncovered so much gold.

Schliemann wanted to dig in the olive groves of Cnossus in Crete, but disturbed political conditions in the island prevented any excavations until the Turks had been expelled. Then in 1900 a wealthy Englishman, Sir Arthur Evans, began to uncover the amazing palace of Cnossus, and with it Minoan civilization.

Since then, archeologists have found other palaces and towns in Crete; they locate new ones even today. Mycenaean palaces and tombs also have been excavated at a number of places in Greece. Finds of this sort are the most spectacular evidence discovered by archeologists. More important, however, for chronological purposes is the abundant pottery of the Minoan and Mycenaean worlds, which can be arranged in a relative sequence. Some of this pottery has been found in Syria and Egypt in sites which can be dated with some precision to years B.C.; from this cross-link, together with some Egyptian objects found in the Aegean world, we can establish the general chronology of prehistoric Greece.

Evans was led to dig at Cnossus partly because he wanted further information about some peculiar "hieroglyphic" writing found on seal stones, but in the excitement of unearthing a new civilization he neglected the writing. In 1939, American archeologists excavating at Pylos found a number of clay tablets, which during World War II were safely locked up in the vaults of the Bank of Greece. After the war they were published, and very soon a brilliant young English architect, Michael Ventris, showed that they contained a syllabic script which was used to set down an early form of Greek. Ventris was killed in an automobile accident, but other scholars have followed his lead in deciphering the business records of the Mycenaean palaces, written in Linear B. An earlier type of writing, Linear A, had been used in Minoan times, but this cannot yet be read.

Linear B disappeared along with the palace bureaucracies during the fall of the Mycenaean world. Thereafter the Dark Ages can be explored only with the help of archeological discoveries. Since men of the period were poor and conditions were often insecure, the physical remains of the Dark Ages are very few; even houses have not often been found. But the dead were buried with containers for oil and wine, occasionally bronze swords, and other objects which might prove useful; iron was not much used until the later part of the Dark Ages. The evolution of this pottery through stages called Protogeometric and Geometric illuminates the fundamental qualities of Greek civilization such as harmony, proportion, and the constant perfection of very simple forms and shapes.

The one cemetery which gives us evidence all across the Dark Ages is located just outside the later Dipylon gate of Athens in the "Potter's Quarter" (Kerameikos). Between World War I and World War II German archeologists excavated the cemetery with very great care, the money having been provided by a Philadelphia textile manufacturer; though the finds are not as glowing as those of Schliemann, they have made it possible for us to see the constant evolution and growing skill of Athenian potters. By the 8th century B.C. these craftsmen could make vases 4–5 feet high to stand atop the graves. Like a Homeric epic, which was built with very simple hexameter lines, these Dipylon vases

DAI, Athens

Protogeometric

DAI, Athens

Friedrich Hewicker

Geometric

Dipylon

Athenian Pottery of the Dark Ages

These three vases show a continuous evolution in shape, though the Dipylon vase is five times as high as the Protogeometric example. So too the artists of all three divided their surfaces into horizontal bands and used their decoration to emphasize and integrate the parts of the vase. About 3 centuries, however, separate the first from the last example.

This is a restored drawing of an 8th-century temple model in clay, with a foreporch and a thatch roof over the *megaron*. The wall was apparently made of stone rubble; both wall and roof were covered with a clay wash which was painted.

Perachora I, pl. 9

are masterpieces composed of balanced decoration of limited variations.

Toward the close of the Dark Ages the volume and variety of archeological material expanded markedly in Greece. Some remains of simple shrines have been found, and in clay models one can see the appearance of the first temples. Throughout the Dark Ages the Greeks had made simple clay figurines of oxen and human beings to dedicate to the gods, but now they began to fashion bronze horses and imaginary animals like griffins to decorate great kettles. Schematic, abstract figurines of warriors in bronze have also been found in religious sanctuaries, which suggest a growing interest in sculpture. In addition, by the end of the Dark Ages the alphabet was being used; great events could be preserved in written, rather than oral, accounts.

Much of early Greek development remains dark to us, for archeologists cannot uncover the actual thoughts, the dreams, and the religious beliefs of men. Only the physical remains of their actions can survive. But we can at least see the general course of development in the early

A small bronze figurine of a warrior,
found on the Acropolis at Athens.
Originally he held a spear in his hand.

Aegean world, with its peaks and violent upheavals, and against this
background we can visualize more clearly the remarkable outburst of
historical Greek civilization. Each year, too, the archeologists add to
our store of knowledge, and our understanding of early Greece is
deepened by patient studies of what has already been found.

The Greeks took over the concept of the griffin from the Near East, but, as in this example from Olympia developed its wicked force into a stylized work of art.

CHAPTER 4

The First Stage
of Greek Civilization

The Inheritance from the Past ▨▨▨▨▨▨▨▨▨▨▨▨▨▨▨▨▨▨▨▨▨
The ancestors of Cleon, Pericles, and all their fellow citizens had
lived in Athens for many generations. The Athenians, indeed, boasted
they had always been there, that is, their stock had not come from
anywhere else and had not been upset in the dim migrations of the
past. They knew too that they inherited their outlook on government
and life from their forefathers; especially they revered the old poems
of Homer as the earliest and best expression of Greek values.

Nowadays many of us are inclined to imagine that the views we
hold about our world are brand new. Some men in Cleon's own day
would have shared the opinion that "Everything is changing; we owe
nothing to the past—at least nothing that is good." Yet we do often
look like our parents, and more than we may realize our attitudes
come from them (or in reaction against them, which is also a form
of indebtedness). The historian is one who admits this fact and goes
on to feel that, if he is to understand a person or a situation, he must
look at its background in the past. This does not mean the historian
believes our actions are totally determined by our inheritance; he
simply knows that the ways of life and thought evolved in past generations are very likely to have a significant effect on what we do in
the present.

So, if we are to understand Cleon and Pericles fully, we must now look back behind 440 B.C. into earlier Greek history. By this date the main characteristics of their civilization had been in existence for at least five centuries, and people who spoke Greek had lived in Greece even longer. Over most of this period we must skip briefly, but at a few important and famous points we must stop for at least a little while.

The Beginnings

From finds in caves we know the earliest men in the Greek landscape long hunted for all of their food. Before 6000 B.C., however, they had learned to farm and had settled down in agricultural villages. Across the next several thousand years the main developments were the result of influences from two different directions. From the Near East, which developed much more rapidly than the Aegean, came ideas and techniques. From the great reaches of uncivilized Europe migrant barbarians trickled down in several distinct waves.

Agriculture itself seems to have been a Near Eastern discovery; so too were the making of pots, bronze working, and other skills which men in the Aegean picked up. The narrow fields of Greece could not provide the rich agricultural surplus afforded by the river valleys of Mesopotamia and Egypt, so down to 2000 B.C. the Aegean world remained quite backward. Still, most sites which were later important had been settled by 2000 B.C., and many cities and mountains kept non-Greek names in later times (just as Indian names stud the map of the United States).

Since the early inhabitants of Greece could not write, we cannot follow their history closely. In particular it is difficult to determine when outsiders came down from the north; in fact, though, this may have happened on several occasions. The most important and most certain invasion arrived in the last centuries before 2000 B.C., when many settlements were burned and lay vacant for a while. Very probably these invaders spoke an early form of Greek; about the same time barbarians with kindred languages poured down across the Near East all the way to India. In mainland Greece the population shrank in the shock of the upheaval, outside contacts by sea were reduced, and the invaders built great rock fortresses on hilltops at Mycenae and elsewhere to dominate the countryside.

Only the upper half of this Minoan vase in steatite (a soft stone) is preserved. A group of harvesters marches home, flails over their shoulders, singing at the top of their lungs to the accompaniment of a musical rattle. Compare the naturalism and joy in life of this vase with the next one, from Mycenaean times.

Minoan Civilization

Between 2000 and 1000 B.C. marvelous advances took place in the Aegean world, only to die away again just before 1000 in another great collapse. The developments that took place on the island of Crete are called Minoan civilization and those that came next on the Greek mainland, Mycenaean civilization.

The long, thin island of Crete evidently had not been upset by the earlier invasions of the mainland, and by 2000 its inhabitants were ready to blaze forth in one of the most attractive civilizations which has ever existed. The impetus came from contemporary progress in the Near East, but nowhere else did artists and craftsmen follow quite the same course. At Cnossus, Phaestus, and elsewhere the kings of the Minoan civilization erected palaces around central courtyards.

These palaces even had baths and drains, and the walls of major rooms were decorated with lovely, naturalistic paintings on plaster (frescoes). Ivory figurines, decorated vases, and other luxurious wares were made with great skill.

Minoan culture gets its name from a legendary king, Minos of Crete. Although it began to be discovered only in 1900, its fresh artistic spirit has given it great popularity. Minoan achievements, however, are not Greek in the way we define "Greek civilization" in history; they must be appreciated for themselves.

Mycenaean Civilization

Historically, the main importance of Minoan culture is the fact that it served as an intermediary between the old civilizations of the Near East and the still-barbarous inhabitants of mainland Greece. Soon after 1600 B.C. those invaders who had conquered Greece earlier began to come into contact with the advanced culture on Crete. The result was the first flicker of civilized life on the European continent. This we call the Mycenaean age, after its greatest center at Mycenae; its dates are roughly 1600–1200 B.C.

Mycenaean culture was limited to a handful of great palaces which were mostly built within the earlier fortresses. The first of these to be discovered were at Mycenae and the nearby seacoast site of Tiryns. Others existed on the Acropolis at Athens, under the modern town of Thebes, at Iolkos in Thessaly, and at Pylos in the western Peloponnesus. These palaces were decorated with frescoes in the Minoan style and they had plumbing. Their architectural center was not a courtyard, as in Minoan buildings, but a great hall with columns and porch in front (the *megaron* of the Homeric poems, and the source of the temple plan).

At Mycenae the rulers were at first buried in graves cut down into the rock, which were grouped within ornamental circles; but by the 15th and 14th centuries B.C. monarchs constructed great *tholos* tombs in the nearby hillside. A *tholos* has an entryway that leads into a tombchamber in domed shape, all constructed from carefully cut stone blocks (the Athenian Tholos, where the Council of 500 met, borrowed only the round shape). The Mycenaean *tholos* tomb called the Treasury of Atreus still stands as the first great architectural work in Europe. Soon thereafter the walls of Mycenae itself were rebuilt, and an ornamental gate of large squared blocks was decorated with a relief of two lions upholding a pillar.

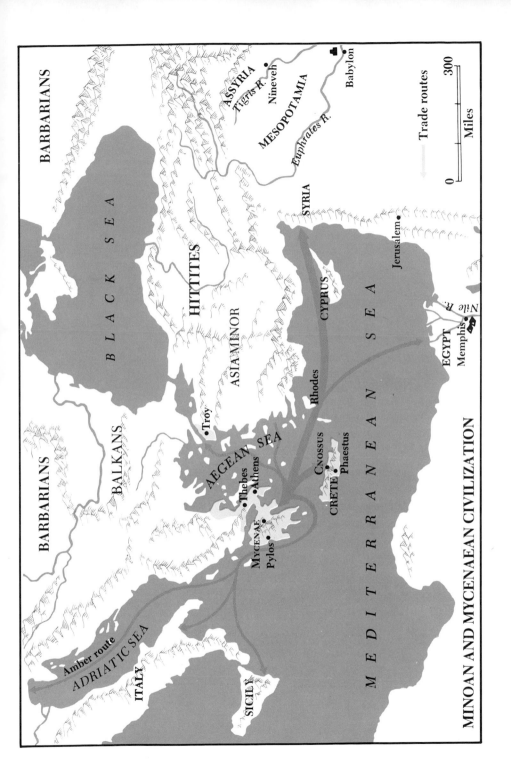

MINOAN AND MYCENAEAN CIVILIZATION

BARBARIANS

BARBARIANS

BLACK SEA

ASSYRIA
Tigris R.
Nineveh •

MESOPOTAMIA

Euphrates R.

Babylon •

HITTITES

ASIA MINOR

SYRIA

Jerusalem •

CYPRUS

Rhodes •

BALKANS

Troy •

AEGEAN SEA

Thebes •
Athens •

Mycenae •
Pylos •

Cnossus •
CRETE • Phaestus

M E D I T E R R A N E A N   S E A

EGYPT
Memphis •
Nile R.

Amber route

ADRIATIC SEA

ITALY

SICILY

→ Trade routes

0   300
Miles

This Mycenaean vase appears top-heavy in shape. Its subject is hard to understand: two people in a chariot approach a figure who holds a scales (is he Zeus, weighing out their destinies?). The horses and men are merely symbols applied to the surface of the vase.

Around the palace-fortresses were villages of peasants, who worked for the Mycenaean princes. Close at hand, at least at Mycenae, were houses of craftsmen who worked in ivory, bronze, and precious metals largely on Minoan models. Each principality had a little bureaucracy, which kept financial records for the king on clay tablets, very much as in Cretan and Near Eastern kingdoms. Some of these tablets in a script called Linear B were accidentally baked when the palaces were burned and have thus survived; they can now be read and it turns out that they were written in a very early form of Greek.

Mycenaean pottery has been found all the way from Sicily to the Near East, for the Mycenaean lords were wide-ranging traders and looters. They conquered Cnossus in Crete by about 1450 and ended the independence of the Minoan world; shortly before 1200, according to legend, they made an attack on Troy in northwestern Asia

THE RISE OF GREEK CIVILIZATION

Minor. This event was remembered and in later days was expanded into the Homeric epic poems (the *Iliad* and the *Odyssey*).

When this attack on Troy took place, the Mycenaean world was already tottering. If one can believe Greek myths at all, its kings fought each other fiercely; the subject population, exploited to furnish labor and food, may have been rebellious; folk memory also told of a wave of barbaric invaders from the north called the Dorians. At any rate the Mycenaean palace of Thebes had been completely destroyed by about 1300; that of Pylos was burned about 1200; Mycenae seems to have held out another 50 years. Thereafter the use of writing and the advanced arts of Mycenaean times disappeared along with the political and economic centralization of the palaces. The population of Greece decreased tremendously in this breakdown, and in many areas only nomads could survive.

The Dark Ages ▨▨▨▨▨▨▨▨▨▨▨▨▨▨▨▨▨▨▨▨▨▨▨▨▨▨▨▨▨▨▨▨
From 1100 to almost 700 B.C. the Greeks had very few foreign contacts. The Aegean basin was cut off from the outside world and people in it existed on a very primitive level. Yet this period, called the Dark Ages, was the era in which the Greeks established the basic lines of their historic civilization politically, religiously, artistically, and intellectually.

Before the Dark Ages the Greeks, for instance, wrote in the syllabic script of Mycenaean tablets; by 700 they had developed from its Phoenician origin an alphabet which is the ancestor of ours. In Mycenaean times the political centers were absolute kings in their palaces; by 700 the simple tribes of the Dark Ages were giving way to the tight bonds of the *polis,* in which all citizens had duties and rights. Mycenaean vases had a high center of gravity, like Minoan pottery, and their columns were larger at the top than at the bottom. Greek vases by 700 had a more stable appearance and were developing an elegance of shape and skill in decoration which led on to the great achievements of Corinthian and Athenian pottery. So too the columns of the Parthenon are larger at the base and taper gracefully to the top.

During the Mycenaean period very different languages had evidently been spoken in the Aegean world; by 700 almost every corner, except for a few backward regions, spoke some form of the Greek language. In the pottery, the simple figurines, the grammar of Greek,

Alison Frantz

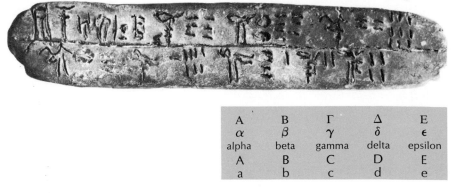

A	B	Γ	Δ	E
α	β	γ	δ	ε
alpha	beta	gamma	delta	epsilon
A	B	C	D	E
a	b	c	d	e

Greek Writing

Above is a Mycenaean tablet from Cnossus in Linear B. This was a script with about 89 symbols for syllables plus specific symbols for men, sheep, and so on. On this tablet the first six signs in the top row are syllables; then come symbols for animals and numbers, as follows: Ram 60, Ewe 270, He-goat 49, [bottom line] She-goat 130, Boar 17, Sow 41, Bull 2, Cow 4. Can you figure out the number system?

Below is a part of the Greek alphabet of historic times (an example of a book on papyrus will be found on page 44, an inscription on stone on page 194). The Greeks took over the shapes and names of their 24 letters from the Phoenician script but used several of the signs to represent vowels (which the Phoenicians did not write). As a result the Greeks could write poetry or anything else with great accuracy, and the script was much easier to learn than Linear B had been.

and in the remaking of the alphabet alike one can see some of the most fundamental characteristics of later Greek civilization—its ability to analyze a problem into basic components and then to synthesize the components to form an answer; its emphasis on harmony and proportion (as we have understood these qualities ever since); and its primary interest in man.

Since there was no writing in the Dark Ages, proper and organized states did not yet exist, we cannot reconstruct clearly the development across these four centuries. Clearly the origins of historic Greek civilization were primarily native. The invaders from the north brought no major ideas with them, and contact with the Near East had been largely broken. The main influence from outside the period itself came from the Mycenaean world, but as we have just seen this inheritance was greatly simplified in the breakdown of the My-

Beside myth and epic the Greeks developed the animal fable, a short story in which animals act like human beings to illustrate their weaknesses. Many fables were attributed to the legendary Aesop, who appears here with a fox.

Fototeca Unione

cenaean age and then was altered extensively. The greatest products of the Dark Ages proper, which have influenced mankind ever since, show this creative process beautifully; these are Greek mythology and the Homeric epics.

Myth and Epic 🔁🔁🔁🔁🔁🔁🔁🔁🔁🔁🔁🔁🔁🔁🔁🔁🔁🔁🔁🔁🔁🔁🔁🔁🔁🔁🔁🔁🔁
Many peoples of the world have created stories about gods and heroes, and these tales, whether coming from India, Greece, or Scandinavia, often have the same basic plot or theme. The most influential mythology of Western civilization, however, has been that created by the Greeks. This stands out above all others for its rich, yet disciplined, imagination; for its humane quality, which rarely emphasized the cruel or frightening aspects of life; and for its esthetic nature. Since the beginning of Greek history, mythology has been a fertile source of ideas for dramatists, artists, and philosophers.

In some few cases Greek mythology borrowed Near Eastern tales; but for the most part it was of native root, and may even at points have had Mycenaean origins. Myths at times were no doubt created to entertain; frequently they had the more serious ends of releasing the tensions of human fallibility, of explaining natural (or unnatural) phenomena, and of crystallizing religious views. The making of myth was a simple, unconscious process which continued into historic times, though then efforts were largely devoted to systematization and rationalization. The major tales seem clearly to have been known by the time of Homer, who refers to several of them.

Throughout Greek mythology there runs a consistent view of the world as dominated by gods who were human save in their greater power and immortality. Essentially these gods were favorable to men, especially to the great heroes. One such hero was Theseus, who traveled to Crete and battled with the Minotaur in the Labyrinth. The tale of Theseus suggests dim memories of Minoan civilization, for the Labyrinth is literally the "house of the double ax," a motif often marked on Cretan walls or designed in gold and silver as a religious symbol. But the story goes on to tell of Theseus' return to Athens, where he became an enlightened administrator over a tidy *polis*. Another great figure was Heracles, who labored to rid the Peloponnesus of various monsters.

The same views which created Greek mythology were also present in the Greek epic, but there they were developed even further into one of the world's greatest literary achievements. For generations entertainers recited stories at the banquets of Dark Age warriors; very popular were tales about the Greek heroes who went to Troy in pursuit of the fair Helen, who had been stolen from her husband Menelaus at Sparta by the cunning Paris. Apart from the fact that Troy was once attacked (probably in the 13th century B.C.), none of the Trojan story is necessarily "true" in the historical sense, but the epic poets and their audiences believed it just as we can believe fairy tales in our youth. Steadily the events of the war and the return home of its heroes were elaborated and told in a simple verse form.

This was the hexameter line (6 poetic feet with very limited variations), which was easy to remember and in which poets could make up their descriptions as they proceeded. Across the centuries the poets also evolved an artificial vocabulary and stock phrases such as "the well-greaved Achaeans" or even whole passages of several lines which described the washing of hands before dinner, the ceremony of sacrifice, and the like; these the poet could recite while his mind was recalling the next action. About one-third of the *Iliad* and *Odyssey* consists of these phrases, often repeated several times.

The *Iliad* and *Odyssey* 🪷🪷🪷🪷🪷🪷🪷🪷🪷🪷🪷🪷🪷🪷🪷🪷🪷🪷🪷🪷🪷🪷

Early in the 8th century B.C., just before the end of the Dark Ages, one of the world's greatest poets, called Homer, took a part of these tales and made them into a long epic, the *Iliad*. The *Iliad* is not the story of the whole Trojan war but is concentrated on the anger of the hero Achilles, when his slave woman, a prize of valor, is taken away by King Agamemnon of Mycenae (brother of Menelaus and leader of the Greek kings). As a result of Achilles' refusal to fight thereafter with his fellow Achaeans, the Trojans almost succeed in seizing and burning the ships of the Greeks; Achilles' best friend Patroclus puts on his armor and goes out to battle, only to be killed by the great Trojan warrior Hector. Then Achilles returns to the fray and avenges Patroclus by killing Hector.

One might expect the story to stop with Achilles' great funeral to Patroclus, but Homer goes on to tell that Achilles is induced by the gods to return the body of Hector to his father Priam so that Hector in turn may be properly buried. The *Iliad* is a tale of passion, of bloody warfare, and of strongly defined, proud heroes. Yet its ultimate lessons are far deeper. Achilles learns the folly of blind anger; the poem is infused with a penetrating sympathy; and man, although great in his military glory, is subject to higher authority. While the gods control what men do, sometimes in detail, at the same time the heroes are free to act as they will—but they must take the consequences.

Some scholars think that the same poet composed both *Iliad* and *Odyssey;* but it appears likely that a second poet, who also went under the name of Homer, used other epic tales about a generation later to form the *Odyssey*, a story of the trials of the wily Odysseus on his return from Troy. This is a tale of adventure far outside the Aegean into lands of fable. Other poets eventually created epic poems about other events in the Trojan war, but only the *Iliad* and *Odyssey* were considered truly great.

As one Athenian wrote, "my father, anxious that I should become a good man, made me learn all the poems of Homer." For here was a great range of heroes, some with crafty tricks, others blunt in honesty, all quick to anger but open to reasoned appeals. The greatest works ever composed in the Greek language came at the very beginning of historic times, though at the end of a long development across the Dark Ages.

The Epic in Art

For centuries Greek artists illustrated events of the Trojan epics, just as medieval sculptors drew inspiration from the Bible. Some of the scenes are of great events, but others show the Homeric heroes in moments of leisure or lesser known activities. If one put together the thousands of pictures, one could almost make an *Iliad* just in illustrations.

Achilles and Ajax gamble with dice. Achilles says *tesara* (4); Ajax, *tria* (3). The vase is a black-figure masterpiece of the painter Exekias soon after 550; notice the skillfully portrayed difference in pose of the two heroes and their rich robes.

Ecole française d'Athènes

The Trojan horse, loaded with Greek warriors, waiting to be dragged on its wheels into Troy (7th-century relief vase from Myconos)

Odysseus and his companions blind the Cyclops so they can escape from his cave (7th-century vase from Argos)

Time Chart No. 2: Greece, 7000-700 B.C.

B.C.	Aegean Developments	Parallel Events in the Near East
7000	Agricultural villages	Beginning of agriculture
6000		Use of pottery
	Use of pottery	
5000		
4000		
		Civilization in Egypt and Mesopotamia
3000		Pyramids
		End of Old Kingdom (Egypt)
	Invasions	Invasions
2000		
	Minoan Culture	Hammurabi's code of laws
1600	**Mycenean Culture**	
		Egyptian Empire
1200	Attack on Troy	Migration of Hebrews
	Invasions	Invasions
1000	**Dark Ages**	
	Protogeometric style	
900		
	Geometric style	
800		Assyrian empire
	Dipylon style/Homer	
	Beginning of colonization	Phoenician colonization
700	**Age of Expansion**	

Summary 🔲🔲🔲🔲🔲🔲🔲🔲🔲🔲🔲🔲🔲🔲🔲🔲🔲🔲🔲🔲🔲🔲🔲🔲🔲🔲🔲🔲🔲
An Athenian like Cleon had only the vaguest view of all that had
happened from 7000 to 700 B.C. Here and there prehistoric walls
stood above ground, as at Mycenae; Cleon thought they had been
made by the giant Cyclops (whence we get the word "cyclopean").
Occasionally a prehistoric tomb was discovered by accident; when
this occurred it was often thought to be the grave of a hero and could
be made the center of a local cult. In myth and epic there lingered
memories of a King Minos and an attack on Troy, but since these
were handed down through the centuries any historical reality they
may have had was long since confused.

Nonetheless very important characteristics of the world in which Cleon lived had been set in this distant past. Most of the crops and animals known to him were present then, and agriculture had become a standard way of life. The working of metals, stone, and clay for artistic and useful purposes had progressed; during the Dark Ages smiths learned how to make iron as well as bronze. Seafarers had traveled widely in Mycenaean days, and the use of the sea had not totally disappeared; by 700 the Greeks were again out in the broad Mediterranean, trading and colonizing over its shores.

Most important of all, the dim centuries of the Dark Ages just before 700 had seen a consolidation of the fundamental framework of later Greek life and history. Its social institutions, such as the family and clan and masculine domination, had been set; the political system called the *polis* was already in existence by 700. The Homeric epics reveal the religious and moral outlook which we term Greek; so too the qualities later to be elaborated in Greek art were already present in the pottery and figurines of the Dark Ages.

5

Greek History, 700-440 B.C.

Age of Expansion. The first major period in Greek civilization is the Dark Ages, 1100–700 B.C., which we have just considered. The second era is the Age of Expansion, which covers the period from just before 700 down to 500 B.C. Then comes the Classical period from 500 to 323.

In this section we shall concentrate on the 7th and 6th centuries but shall come down into the 5th century far enough to meet Cleon in 440.

The Age of Expansion is marked by a great outburst in every aspect of life and culture. The population of Greece had risen across the Dark Ages, and from 750 on, people moved out of the Aegean in great waves. In the less civilized areas to the north and west the Greeks settled along the coasts of the Black and Mediterranean seas and created new states which eventually spread their civilization over much of Europe. These are the famous Greek colonies, but one must always remember a Greek "colony" was normally an absolutely independent *polis*. Its only lasting ties with its mother state were religious and cultural.

The Near East was relatively very civilized and by this time was controlled by the Assyrian empire and Egypt. Here the Greeks could establish only trading posts, where they picked up the alphabet, better ways of making clay figurines from molds, ideas on sculpture, and skills in working metal objects. Thereafter Greece and the Near

East came more and more closely in contact until Alexander the Great conquered the Near East.

Politically the Greeks had generally advanced in the 8th century beyond the earlier fairly loose tribal structures and had developed the *polis* as the basic framework of their life. The Aegean world was composed of hundreds of tiny, completely independent political units, atoms as it were, each of which demanded the loyalty of at most a few thousand male citizens. During the Age of Expansion these local political structures became tighter; thereafter the Greek states warred repeatedly with each other over such things as tiny bits of frontier land and insults (see page 79). Artists and writers were stimulated by close ties with their fellow citizens in the *polis,* but these political rivalries made it impossible for the Greeks ever to unite voluntarily. Only many centuries later, when the Romans conquered the eastern Mediterranean, did Greece become a political unit rather than simply a geographical district.

It is true that in the Age of Expansion the Greeks developed great international festivals at the religious shrines of Olympia, Delphi, Delos, and elsewhere, where poets and athletes could rival each other. Both because the Greeks were meeting foreigners overseas and because of these common religious and cultural centers, men of the Aegean became more aware of their "Greekness," but this meant no more politically to an Athenian or Spartan than the idea of being a "European" does today to a German or Frenchman.

Another great development of the Age of Expansion was the evolution of a consciously aristocratic standard of life out of the heroic ways celebrated by Homer. Aristocrats everywhere became more luxurious in daily life, thanks to Near Eastern models, and often exploited their poorer fellow citizens. The development of coinage shortly before 600 quickened economic life and made it easier for the aristocrats to build up economic surpluses.

At the same time the more serious aristocrats felt their duties as warriors, as patrons of culture, and as leaders in the *polis.* The aristocratic way of life, which emphasized elegance, athletic skill, and social responsibility (at least in theory), was eventually passed on from Greece to Rome, from Rome to the Middle Ages, and from the Middle Ages to modern Europe. Down to the last century it set the dominant social values in Western civilization.

GAUL

SPAIN

Massilia

Etruscans

ITALY

Rome

Gades

Straits of Gibraltar
(Pillars of Heracles)

MEDITERRANEAN

See inset map

SICILY

GREEK COLONIZATION IN THE

AGE OF EXPANSION, 750—500 B.C.

Carthage

NORTH

**SOUTHERN ITALY
AND SICILY**

Neapolis

Cumae

Paestum

Tarentum

Sybaris

Croton

Zankle
(Messina)

Acragas

Gela

Syracuse

0   100

Miles

■ Home state
□ Greek colony
★ Greek trading pos
● Non-Greek city

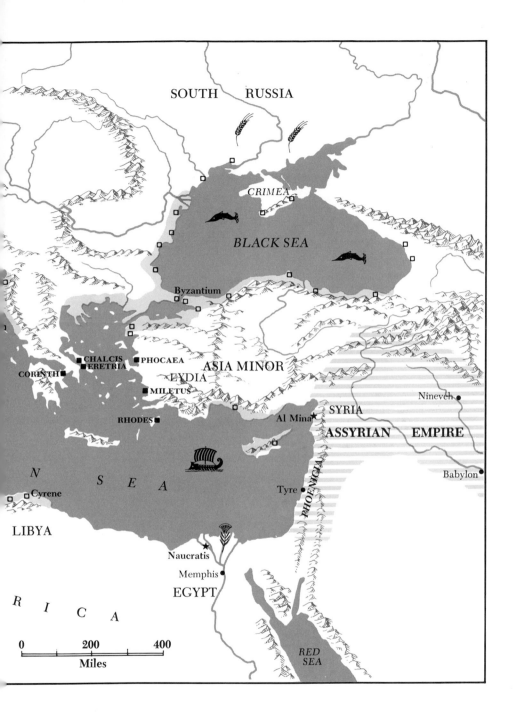

SOUTH RUSSIA

CRIMEA

BLACK SEA

Byzantium

CHALCIS **PHOCAEA** ASIA MINOR
ERETRIA
CORINTH■ LYDIA
■MILETUS

RHODES■ Al Mina★ SYRIA Nineveh ●

ASSYRIAN **EMPIRE**

N *S E A* Babylon ●

●Cyrene Tyre ● PHOENICIA

LIBYA

Naucratis★
Memphis ●
EGYPT

R I C A

0   200   400
Miles

RED
SEA

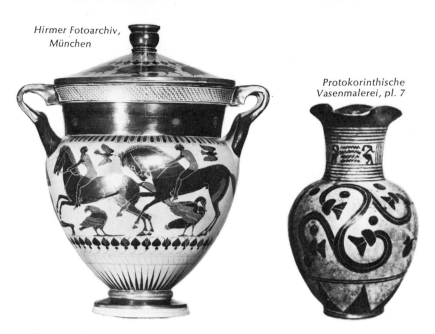

Hirmer Fotoarchiv,
München

Protokorinthische
Vasenmalerei, pl. 7

If you will look back at the Dark Age pottery on page 85, the change which has taken place by the time of these two vases will be more evident. The vase on the right was made about 700 in Corinth, but was found at Cumae in Italy— part of the growing exports to the colonies. The decoration of its neck is still largely Geometric in style, but the floral decoration which sprawls over the belly of the vase suggests the freedom and naturalistic impulses of the "Orientalizing" style (late 8th–early 7th centuries).

The vase on the left is a black-figure product of Chalcis in about 530 and was found north of Rome. It shows two young aristocrats racing on their horses; the birds are included to fill up blank spaces. Note that in ancient times horsemen did not have stirrups.

Literature and Art

These aristocrats encouraged a great development of poetry. The Homeric poets had hidden their own personalities in long epic stories, but about 700 B.C. the poet Hesiod poured out his anger, in epic hexameters, against his brother, who had stolen his father's estate (see page 18). Thereafter poets expressed their own loves and hates in a variety of verse forms, usually in short poems sung to the accompaniment of a lyre. One of the most famous in later times was the only great Greek poetess, Sappho of Lesbos, who wrote poems to her girl pupils and friends about 600 B.C.

As the Greeks began to produce an economic surplus, they poured it into the construction of much larger temples than the simple hut-shrines of the Dark Ages. For daily needs, however, they erected marketplaces with covered walkways, elaborate fountains where the women could draw their daily supply of water, and other buildings. By about 650 the Greeks had begun to carve life-size statues in marble and other stone, which they placed near the temples as aristocratic dedications to the gods. Sometimes the statues represented deities, and at other times aristocratic men and women (see page 133). Sculptors, gem-cutters, coin-designers, potters, and metal-workers all had become more technically skillful and artistically supple than ever; by 500 B.C. Greek artistic products were popular all over the Mediterranean.

The Greatness of Philosophy

When we look back at the Age of Expansion, we see that one of its most remarkable and unexpected achievements was the emergence of rational, disciplined, man-centered thought. This development led to the appearance of written history, to medical treatises, to geometry, and above all to what the Greeks called "philosophia." Literally this word means "love of wisdom," but it came to signify especially a rational exploration of the nature and origins of the world (which we would call "science") and also of the place of man in the world (which we would call strictly "philosophy").

The first "philosopher" was Thales of Miletus, who lived just after 600 B.C. Like many Greeks he loved to talk in the marketplace, and he advanced the idea that the whole world had developed out of water by purely natural processes. The idea seems absurd to us; the important point is his assertion that the evolution had been natural, not god-directed. Thereafter one man after another took up the problem of the origins of the world and relentlessly criticized his predecessors, while advancing new ideas of his own.

One of the most famous philosophers was Pythagoras, who left his native island of Samos to avoid the Persians and settled at Croton in south Italy shortly before 500 B.C. Pythagoras is known to every student of geometry for his proof that the square of the hypotenuse of a right-angled triangle is equal to the sum of the squares of the other two sides (the fact had long been known, but his theoretical proof is the beginning of Greek geometric thought). He also discov-

Was this man a philosopher? Not necessarily: Pericles and Themistocles both had beards; but certainly he looks as though he was a serious thinker. This seal was carved in jasper by Dexamenos of Chios for use by some 5th-century aristocrat (the photograph is an enlargement of a cast of the seal for greater clarity).

Boston, Museum of Fine Arts

ered that the relations of musical notes can be expressed as mathematical ratios; from this discovery he jumped—as Greek philosophers often did—to the idea that the whole universe was a harmonious structure best understood in geometrical terms. A Pythagorean wise man spent his time getting his soul "in tune" with this infinite harmony, which produced the "music of the spheres" (or planets); if successful he could avoid the transmigration of his soul.

These Pythagorean ideas illustrate very important aspects of early Greek thinking. Much of it was illogical, even superstitious: men who were too ignorant to understand Pythagorean harmonics and geometry could save themselves by avoiding certain taboos, such as eating beans. We hear also of ascetics and religious fanatics, for in this great age of upheaval, which produced sudden, unexpected changes in men's fortunes, many feared the gods. The god Apollo gave wise advice to "know thyself" (i.e., to realize one's human limitations) at his oracle of Delphi and became very popular as a way of finding out the divine will. Other men and women turned to emotional orgies, particularly those in the worship of the god Dionysus, to liberate them from their fears.

Yet most Greeks were confident enough not to fall into religious terrors and freeze their lives in superstition. Politically they reorganized and strengthened the public machinery of their government. Economically they built up a surplus which could be used for great buildings; the arts steadily expanded. So too, from the days of Thales on, Greek thinkers developed their ideas. The philosophers were not much interested in experiments, although when they found a fact they often, like Pythagoras, drew very wide conclusions from it. Mostly they talked and argued. In doing so they made clearer the fundamental philosophical problems involved in the concepts of existence, of change, and of natural development.

By the middle of the 5th century B.C. the philosopher Empedocles had advanced the idea that the fundamental elements of the universe were four (earth, air, fire, and water), which were moved by the opposing forces of Love and Strife. Medical men drew from this the theory that man's health depended on a balance of four "humors" (blood, air, yellow bile, black bile). Such ideas, as well as many others of the Greeks, were dominant in European thinking past the time of Shakespeare, who talked seriously of "the music of the spheres"; today we still speak in terms of being in good or bad humor. Another line of thought, which was less favored, was advanced by the philosopher Democritus, that the world was made up of indivisible small particles called "atoms," which were self-moved without any divine guidance.

Many solutions to the problems of the philosophers were proposed. What is really important in early Greek philosophy are: first, the conscious development of logic; second, the belief that man can comprehend his world and that it is governed by rational laws; third, the tradition of free inquiry which takes nothing as sacred and beyond question.

The Power of Sparta
Earlier in this book we looked carefully at the way an Athenian citizen lived and thought around 440 B.C. Frequently the historian must concentrate his attention on one great leader or one important period, but when he does he runs the danger that his readers will think this is the *only* thing that happened. Athens was merely one of more than

Hirmer Fotoarchiv, München

A great Spartan plate: King Arcesilas of Cyrene sits on the deck of a ship while traders weigh out silphium, a famous medicinal plant of ancient North Africa. Below, other workers pile up the sacks in the hold for shipment. The lizard and monkey also suggest the geographic background.

a hundred states in mainland Greece; to take it as typical is like saying England is typical of all Europe. During the Age of Expansion, indeed, Athens was much less important than Sparta.

In 700 B.C. Sparta and Athens were very much alike. They both still had kings as war chieftains but were developing conscious aristocracies. Of the two, Sparta seems to have advanced more rapidly in the 7th century. Great quantities of carved ivory have been found at a major Spartan religious shrine of Artemis, and Spartan pottery had been exported widely throughout the Mediterranean at a time when Athenian pottery had fallen into a stylistic slump and could be sold only at home. The Spartans were also famous all over the

Aegean for their choruses of maidens and men; great poets of choral lyrics, similar to oratorios, flourished at Sparta in the 7th century.

The Spartans led in putting ultimate political power in the hands of a citizen Assembly; in Sparta the Assembly was guided by a steering Council of 30 Elders (28 elected plus the 2 kings). The members of this Assembly came from the villages on the fertile plain of the Eurotas river; in the hills lived citizens who could not vote, called the *perioikoi* (dwellers-about).

Eventually the Spartans came to have a unique pattern of life. In the valley of the Eurotas the citizen body dominated small peasants, called "helots," who were tied permanently to the land, and instead of colonizing extensively the Spartans added more helots by conquering their neighbors in Messenia shortly before 700. In 640 the Messenian helots revolted in a bitter war which took 20 years to put down. During the following years the Spartan citizens reorganized their way of living, government, and army to be sure they would always be strong enough to keep the helots in subjection. This reorganization took place slowly, but the Spartans themselves attributed many of the reforms to a legendary figure named Lycurgus. The end result was the "Lycurgan system," in which service to the state and concentration on the military virtues of physical prowess, courage, and discipline were more emphasized than they were in any other Greek *polis*.

The Spartan Way of Life When a boy was born in a Spartan family, state inspectors decided whether he looked strong enough to grow·up to be a warrior. If he did, his mother raised him until he was 7, at which time he and other boys of the same age were put in a "pack" governed by teenage youths. Each pack engaged in physical training and ate and dressed simply. To supplement their restricted diet and to teach them how to live off the countryside, boys were encouraged to steal, but they were heavily beaten if they were caught. Youths waited on the tables of the adult warriors, where they could hear songs and tales of bravery. At 20 the young men were placed in military squads of 15 each and lived and fought with their fellow squad members for the next 10 years; the food for their messes was provided by helots, each citizen having an allotment of land with helots to cultivate it.

Usually boys got married soon after reaching manhood, but they could not live permanently with their wives until after they were 30.

Even then, men were in the "ready reserve" and had to be prepared to go off and fight at a moment's notice. So Spartan women were remarkably free to direct the farms and govern their families. They too, as girls, were encouraged to engage in physical activities such as running so that they could be strong mothers.

The Spartan citizens themselves were called "the Equals," for in theory all were equal in war and government. The two kings served as war chieftains; the Council of Elders and Assembly made the decisions; and a Board of 5 Ephors, elected annually, checked the kings and the general conduct of politics.

Sparta Abroad

Throughout the 6th century the Spartan kings used their fine military machine not only to keep down the helots but also to conquer most of the Peloponnesus; only the strong state of Argos remained completely independent. But the Spartans did not want to add more helots to their state, and so they made the Arcadians and others dependent allies. Late in the 6th century the great Spartan king Cleomenes organized these allies firmly into the Peloponnesian league. Each *polis* sent representatives to a council which met near the Spartan assembly; only if both bodies voted in favor of a policy could it then be carried out by the Spartan kings.

Most of us probably would rather have lived in Athens than in Sparta; but many of the greatest Greek thinkers such as Plato (an Athenian himself) much preferred Sparta. Sparta was stable; the Athenian democracy was restless and unpredictable. The Spartans were devoted to their community and emphasized physical virtues; Athenians were noted for being quarrelsome and money-seeking (the Spartans did not even coin money). Modern students often point out that Sparta lost the cultural leadership it had held in the 7th century and they attribute this to the growing Spartan "militarism," but actually Greek culture came to be centered on Athens in the 5th century largely because all trade routes had then begun to lead there.

In foreign policy particularly, one needs to think carefully about the effect of Spartan policies. The Spartans gave their allies much more voice than did the Athenians to their subjects, and did not exact tribute; they were in reality far less imperialistic than were the followers of Pericles. Apart from keeping down the helots at home, the main objectives of Spartan policy from 600 to 400 B.C. were to prevent any state in Greece from becoming dangerous and to bar any outsider from entering the Aegean world. Time and time again other Greeks appealed to Sparta for help; even the Athenians did so in 510 in order to get rid of their tyrant Hippias.

When the greatest outside threat came from the Persian empire, just after 500, those Greeks who were willing to fight chose Sparta voluntarily as their leader; and thanks in part to Spartan discipline and its well-trained army the Greeks won, though barely, the decisive battles against the Persians. Sparta, in sum, represents almost as important a part of Greek civilization as Athens does.

The Background of the Persian Wars

To understand this Persian attack we must go back again into earlier history. During the Dark Ages and the Age of Expansion, as we have just seen, the Aegean world had almost no political contacts abroad, so the tiny Greek states had an opportunity to consolidate their culture and political strengths. In the Near East, which was much more advanced economically and politically, the Assyrians built up a great empire, but it did not extend far into Asia Minor. After the fall of the Assyrian empire in 612 B.C., there was a brief period in which the Near East was divided. Then a local Persian king, Cyrus, united the vigorous lords who ruled in the Iranian mountain valleys and began to conquer the Near East in 550. During the following years he went farther than the Assyrians had gone and annexed the kingdom of Lydia, ruled by its famous king Croesus. The Persians were now in control of the Greeks on the east coast of the Aegean.

Cyrus' son Cambyses took Egypt and then died mysteriously. A civil war followed, which a distant relative Darius won in 522. Darius was the real organizer of the Persian empire into provinces or "satrapies"; he built a great secluded fortress-treasury at Persepolis and struck coins, the famous gold "darics." From 512 to 492 his generals extended Persian rule into Europe along the north coast of the Aegean as far as Macedonia.

In 499 the Greek states in Asia Minor revolted and asked for help from their free Greek cousins across the Aegean. The Spartans thought over the appeal and wisely refused to commit their army so far afield; but two Greek states, Athens and Eretria, gave a little

The Persian Majesty

Persepolis was built on a terrace twice the size of the Acropolis. It was equipped with a maze of staircases, palaces, audience halls, and other buildings; here the "king of kings" could feel he was "king of this great earth far and wide," as his inscriptions boast.

Two staircases were decorated with exactly the same scenes of tribute-bearers. These are probably Cilicians with prize sheep. The vigor of the decoration may be due to Greek workmen, but they were not encouraged to enliven the rather tubular, simplified bodies. Contrast the Parthenon relief shown on page 75.

Time Chart No. 3: Persia and Greece

B.C.	Major Events
550	Cyrus begins Persian expansion
525	Cambyses takes Egypt
512, on	Darius takes north coast of Aegean Cleomenes reorganizes Peloponnesian league
499	Greek revolt in Asia Minor
494	Destruction of Miletus
490	✗ Marathon
480	Themistocles builds Athenian fleet ✗ Thermopylae ✗ Cape Artemisium ✗ Salamis
479	✗ Plataea ✗ Mycale
478	Delian league formed for revenge Expulsion of Persians from Aegean
449	Athenian peace with Persia

help for a brief while—too little to be useful but enough to cause great troubles to Greece. Within five years the Persians put down the revolt, partly because the rebel Greeks could not agree on a single leader. Then they destroyed the greatest of the cities, Miletus, as a warning.

King Darius decided further to punish Athens and Eretria and sent a small expedition across the Aegean by ship in 490. It duly destroyed Eretria and then landed on Athenian territory at Marathon. The Athenians hurried their famous distance runner, Phidippides, to Sparta to beg aid, but before the Spartan army could arrive the Athenians themselves had succeeded in defeating the Persians on land. (According to tradition, Phidippides ran back to Athens and announced the victory as he collapsed; he was the first "Marathon runner.")

Themistocles (a Roman copy)

Xerxes' Invasion

To Darius this setback must have appeared to be one of those little frontier difficulties which every empire must expect. He decided to expand his operations and conquer all of mainland Greece. Before his army and navy could get ready, Darius died, and his son Xerxes was delayed by a revolt in Egypt. Once the revolt was put down, Xerxes went to Asia Minor (in the fall of 481) and prepared to gain the glory of expanding the Persian empire yet farther at the expense of the Greeks. During the winter 481–480 his army of about 180,000 men and navy of 600-odd ships assembled on the Asia Minor coast. The resulting struggle between the great Persian empire and a tiny band of Greek states is one of the most famous tales of ancient history.

The 10 years following the battle at Marathon had been spent by the mainland Greeks in their usual pastime of fighting each other, but the goddess Athena did bestow two great gifts on her favorite city of Athens. One was the rise of Themistocles, one of the most keen-sighted and persuasive politicians ever produced in Athens. First he managed to have his rivals ostracized so that leadership was undivided in his hands. Then he took advantage of Athena's second gift, the discovery of a very rich level of silver in the state mines of Laurium. Normally the silver would have been divided among the citizens, but Themistocles persuaded them to use it to build a navy of 200 triremes, the largest and best in Greece.

When news of Xerxes' preparations came, most Greek states either went over to the Persians at once or stayed neutral. Some consulted the oracle at Delphi; Apollo calculated the odds and in veiled language counseled surrender. The Athenians, however, were not to be given the chance to yield, and the Spartans refused to do so.

In a meeting at the isthmus of Corinth in the fall of 481, a small band of fewer than 30 Greek states agreed to fight the Persians. Most important of all, they appointed Sparta commander by land and sea alike. The Greeks could muster a land force only about half the size of the Persian army, but fighter for fighter the Greeks were better armored and disciplined. On the sea the Greeks had a navy about half that of their opponent, and the Phoenician sailors in the Persian service were more skilled than the Greeks at naval maneuvers.

The Battles of 480 and 479
In the spring of 480 Xerxes' army crossed the Hellespont on a bridge of boats and proceeded along the north coast of the Aegean, already Persian territory. The Spartans wanted to fortify the isthmus of Corinth and fight on that narrow strip of land, but Themistocles pointed out that the Persian navy could simply ferry the Persians around behind the wall to Argos, which had remained neutral because it hated Sparta. The real key, in Themistocles' keen view, was the Persian navy; but to deal with it the Greeks had to fight in a narrow body of water where superior numbers and the skill of the Phoenicians would not be useful to the Persians.

The arrangement of such a fight might be possible, for the Persian army and navy had to remain close together. The Persian galleys needed a friendly shore on which to rest their rowers at night, and the Persian army was so large it had to have seaborne supplies rather than live off the land as it advanced. So Themistocles persuaded the Spartans to send the navy to Cape Artemisium, between the island of Euboea and the mainland, and a small army of 9000 men, under the Spartan king Leonidas, to the narrow passage of Thermopylae. If the Greek land forces could hold this pass, the Persian navy would have to come in to attack the Greek fleet in order to open a way for the army.

So it came to pass, and three naval battles were fought to a draw off Cape Artemisium. The Persians meanwhile sent a large detachment around Euboea to bottle up the Greek fleet at its southern end, but a sudden north wind drove the Persian galleys onto the rocky shores of Euboea. Leonidas, too, held the pass—until a Greek traitor showed the Persians a mountain path around behind the Greek army. Leonidas received a warning in time to send off most of his army before it was trapped, but he stayed as a rearguard with his 300 Spartans and a few others. All the Spartans were killed, and the vengeful Xerxes nailed the dead body of Leonidas to a cross.

Nothing could now stop the Persians, who went on to take Athens and burn the Acropolis; the Greek fleet, which had fallen back to Salamis, evacuated the Athenians. Once again the Spartans wanted to make their stand at the isthmus of Corinth; once more Themistocles pointed out that the Greeks had no chance in open waters. After a heated debate Sparta agreed to allow the Greek navy to fight the Persians in the narrow bay of Salamis, if Themistocles could entice them in. He sent a slave who was tutor of his children to Xerxes by night with the message that the Greeks were quarreling and the Athenians were ready to desert.

Xerxes, desiring the military glory of a decisive victory, ordered his fleet (now about equal to the Greeks in size) to attack and himself sat on a throne on a hill overlooking the bay, so he could know who among his captains deserved prizes. The Persians came in but had no chance to use their naval skills. Instead, they soon locked hand to hand with the Greeks, who had loaded their ships with heavy-armed soldiers. In the confused struggle which followed the Persian fleet was crushed.

Xerxes at once scampered back to Asia Minor, but left half his

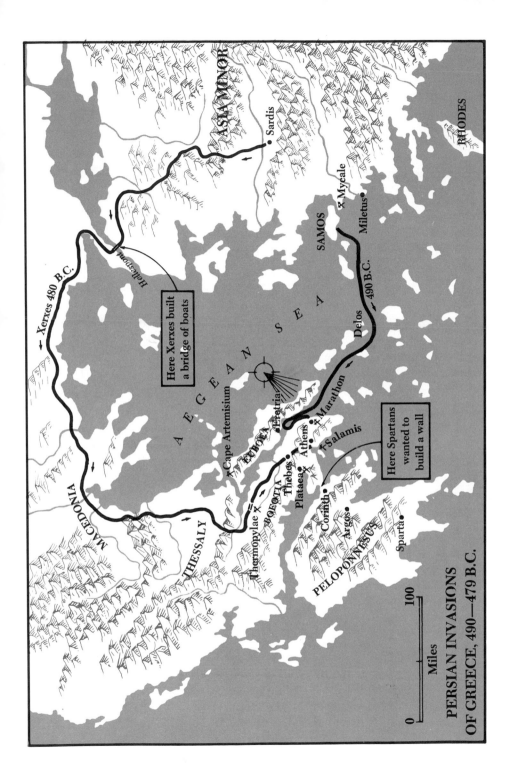

PERSIAN INVASIONS
OF GREECE, 490—479 B.C.

ASIA MINOR

Sardis

RHODES

Mycale
Miletus

SAMS

Xerxes 480 B.C.

Hellespont

Here Xerxes built
a bridge of boats

490 B.C.

Delos

A E G E A N   S E A

Marathon

Cape Artemisium

EUBOEA

Eretria

Here Spartans
wanted to
build a wall

Athens

Salamis

MACEDONIA

Thebes

BOEOTIA

Plataea

Corinth

Thermopylae

THESSALY

Argos

PELOPONNESUS

Sparta

100

Miles

0

army in northern Greece to try for a land victory. In the spring of 479 the Persian commander Mardonius once more invaded Athens, then withdrew across the mountains to Boeotia, where the Spartans had brought up all their army. The Greeks numbered as many as the Persians, and in the battle of Plataea they wiped out the Persian army. About the same time, a naval force destroyed the remnants of the Persian navy on the east coast of the Aegean at Mycale.

Why Did the Greeks Win? The story of the Persian invasions is told to us by the first great historian, Herodotus; there also survives the tragedy, *The Persians*, by Aeschylus, who fought at Marathon and at Salamis. Herodotus and Aeschylus each have a high respect for the Persians' loyalty to their king, although they directly contrast the absolute rule by the Persian despot and Greek freedom. Both, though, see the Greek victory as a sign of divine punishment for the overweening pride (*hybris*) of Xerxes. So the Greeks gave the credit to their gods. The Athenians set up a temple to the North Wind (Boreas), and all the Greeks made dedications at the temple of Apollo at Delphi. One of these, a bronze support for a gold tripod which bore the names of the states fighting the Persians, stands in Istanbul, where it was moved in Christian times.

Human valor did have its place alongside divine aid. All the Greek generals voted as to who was the most worthy after the battle of Salamis; each voted for himself first, and for Themistocles second. Herodotus points out the strategic problems of supply and coordination which the Persians had faced with their huge forces, and as he sums it up, "If the Athenians, through fear of the approaching danger, had abandoned their country, or if they had stayed there and submitted to Xerxes, there would have been no attempt to resist the Persians by sea; and, in the absence of a Greek fleet, it is easy to see what would have been the course of events on land. . . . Next to the gods the Athenians repelled the invaders" by standing firm despite two invasions and by providing the backbone of the allied navy. We today might emphasize as well the solid, unyielding bravery of the Spartans and the willingness of the Greeks to place over-all command in Spartan hands. To Herodotus the Persian wars are an imperishable tale of valor and great deeds; so they are, but they also are studded with jealousy, treachery, and narrow-minded patriotism.

Time Chart No. 4: Greece, 750-440 B.C.

B.C.	Major Events	Artists and Writers
750	Beginning of colonization, rise of *polis* Spartan conquest of Messenia	Late Geometric art
700		Hesiod **Archaic Art** pottery: Corinth, Sparta, etc.
650	Revolt of Messenia	stone temples large-scale sculpture lyric poetry choral poetry (Sparta)
	Beginning of coinage	
600	Solon (Athens)	Sappho Athenian black-figure pottery Thales
550	Cyrus (Persian empire) Pisistratus (Athens)	Pythagoras Xenophanes
		Athenian red-figure pottery
	Darius (Persian empire, conquest of north Aegean Cleomenes (Sparta)	
500		
490		
480	Persian invasion	**Classic Art** Phidias, Polyclitus Aeschylus Pindar Herodotus
	Athenian empire	
	Pericles (Athens)	Sophocles Empedocles, Anaxagoras
450	Peace with Persia	Hippocrates

(left margin vertical text: Age of Expansion)

Delian League and Athenian Empire

After repelling the Persians the Spartans felt they had done enough in terms of their long-range policies. They were ready to quit and urged that the Greeks of Asia Minor be brought over to mainland Greece and settled in the states which had supported the Persians.

The islanders, the Ionians, and the Athenians were not pleased: they wanted vengeance on the Persians.

People from these areas met on the island of Delos in the winter of 478–477 and agreed to form a league to punish the Persians and to prevent their return. The Athenians, the greatest state in the league, furnished a large part of the navy as well as the general-admirals and the treasurers; the small states provided money, the large states ships for a common navy. In the next 30 years the Delian league, for the most part led by the great Athenian commander Cimon, drove the Persians entirely out of the Aegean and went on to help rebels in Cyprus and Egypt.

Gradually and almost unconsciously, as we have already seen, the Athenians converted this voluntary league into an empire under their control. In 449 their negotiator, Callias, made a verbal arrangement for peace with the Persians, who agreed to stay out of the Aegean if the Athenians would stop helping rebels elsewhere. By this time Pericles was already beginning to seek Athenian power over the neighboring states in mainland Greece; but this effort was stopped by the Spartans and Boeotians in a brief war which ended in 446. Then Athens was temporarily at peace everywhere.

Athens in 440 B.C. So, after our long detour through earlier Greek history, we have come back to the age of Cleon and Pericles, with whom we began our story. To Cleon the many centuries before 700 were very dim, and only unconsciously did they influence the way he acted. A number of events and persons after that date, however, directly affected his judgment on internal and external policies. In childhood he learned of Solon the moderate reformer, of Pisistratus the tyrant, of Clisthenes the founder of democracy, and of Themistocles the shrewd.

Cleon deeply distrusted the Persians, who had destroyed his native city in two successive years. If Athens ruled the Aegean, that empire could be justified because of its success in holding back the Persians. To the Spartans, on the other hand, Athenian strength became more and more dangerous; for a cardinal principle in Spartan policy was to keep any Greek state from being too powerful. The peace which the Greek world enjoyed in 440 was only a temporary balance.

Greek Warfare

The Greek Arts

**The Western
Greeks**

GREEK WARFARE

Warfare and civilization developed hand in hand in historic Greece. As the states tightened their internal organization, they fell at odds with each other. Sometimes they quarreled over the control of a religious shrine or for patriotic reasons; sometimes both sides coveted a valuable piece of frontier land. The first great war of which we hear is the Lelantine war, which took place shortly before 700 B.C. It was fought between Chalcis and Eretria (on the island of Euboea) over a tiny plain and went on for years. Wars occurred frequently thereafter.

Homer describes battles in terms of the duels of heroes (though in the background of the Homeric battlefields there also stood masses of infantry). From 700 B.C. on, the closer unity of the *polis* reduced the place of individual fighters, and the infantry was drawn up several men deep in a long battle front. The soldiers of this phalanx, called *hoplites,* were equipped with a bronze helmet, breastplate, greaves (shin guards) on the leg, round shield, spear, and short sword. Light-armed soldiers skirmished on the flanks with javelins, slings, and bows and arrows. Since warriors had to provide their own equipment, only the well-to-do farmers served in the phalanx. Some of the wealthiest might ride to the battlefield on horseback and then dismount to fight on foot.

In a Greek battle both sides lined up on a piece of flat ground, where they could keep their ranks straight, and then drove at each other as serried masses. When the spearsmen of one side gave way and fled,

Hirmer Fotoarchiv, München

Two phalanxes march into battle. The outside of the shields has an emblem; the inside, a hand grip and an elbow strap (which do not show here). The helmets are of the Corinthian type with cheek guards and crests. Behind, a musician pipes on his double oboe; probably the soldiers are chanting a simple song to keep in step and encourage themselves to be brave.

they suffered heavy casualties, because there were no long-range weapons to slow the pursuit. The victorious side, which lost very few men, chased until it got tired, then returned to the battlefield to set up a monument to its prowess and to bury its dead. The role of the generals in this type of fighting was to discover the will of the gods through sacrifice, to decide when to fight, and to encourage their troops before the battle; for maneuver was very limited until the 4th century. Then generals began to make more use of light-armed soldiers (*peltasts*) and varied the depth of their phalanx to seek a decision on one flank or the other.

If a state did not want to fight, it could remain within its walls, where it was virtually safe. Originally, Greek states had only a point of refuge, like the Acropolis at Athens; but by the 5th century major states could afford walls of stone or brick (which had sometimes been built earlier by cities in Asia Minor and in Sicily). The Greeks did not have gunpowder and were not skilled in erecting siege engines such as rams and movable towers, so a siege consisted mostly of starving out a city.

Aegosthenea was a 4th-century fortress in mountainous terrain on the Corinthian gulf. In the tower are windows for machines which discharged arrows and bolts (catapults).

Members of the religious league of Delphi, which included most major Greek states, swore oaths not to poison an enemy's water supply.

When a city fell, the defeated side paid a heavy penalty for keeping the besiegers occupied for month after month or even for years. Usually the adult males were killed, and women and younger children were sold into slavery. Greek vase-painters depicted the horrors of war largely in terms of the terrible punishment of the Trojans; Euripides likewise wrote great tragedies of war in his *Trojan Women* and other plays. Not until the 4th century, however, did the Greeks try to reduce the amount of warfare by making leagues of states and publicizing the advantages of a "common peace." These methods did not work very well, but the treatment of the conquered side did improve.

THE GREEK ARTS

Greek art in the period down to Alexander is divided into two main stages: the Archaic (7th and 6th centuries) and the Classical (5th and 4th centuries). The basic principles of the Greek artistic spirit had already been set in the Dark Ages, but after 700 the growing wealth of the Aegean permitted wider and more extensive artistic activity. In some aspects of techniques the Greeks also learned from the Near East.

If we look at all the forms of art together, there are several important common characteristics. Artistic production of every kind was connected with religion, except in the case of those objects designed for household or public use. The Greek arts also expressed that aristocratic spirit which was dominant in their civilization, although the artists themselves were ordinary craftsmen, not aristocrats. Again, artists in every field concentrated on a few simple forms, often inherited from the Dark Ages, which they steadily refined and polished. As a rule Greek art did not favor that experimentation and breaking away from convention which we find in the arts today; the aim rather was to restrain and civilize the emotions. Finally, Greek artists, like the philosophers, sought to express eternally true ideals. They did not make portraits of specific individuals or spend much time on the casually interesting or humorous.

To support these generalizations, let us consider a few of the arts, first architecture, then sculpture, and more briefly pottery and painting.

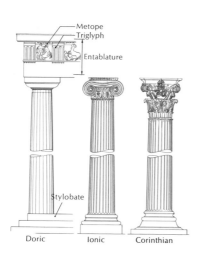

Metope
Triglyph
Entablature
Stylobate

Doric   Ionic   Corinthian

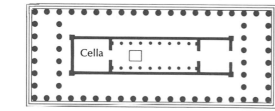

Cella

The Greek Temple

The three main types of columns and the ground plan of a temple are illus-trated in the sketches. A great variety of decoration could also be used in a temple. The lion spouts, through which poured water drained from the roof, were on a Sicilian temple (at Himera). The terracotta figure of the Gorgon with her child, the winged horse Pegasus, may have been placed on a temple (or altar) at Syracuse to ward off evil spirits. As this last work suggests, temples were gaily painted.

In architecture the most important form was the temple, a building designed mainly to protect the statue of a deity. Ordinary citizens did not usually meet inside a temple, so interior space was not important; the object rather was to make a beautiful "box." Most ceremonies took place outside at the altar, which was normally placed at the east end of a temple (oriented east-west if the ground permitted). Other than priests, only treasurers had access to the interior; temples were often the "banks" of a country's reserves.

The basic idea of the temple came from the prehistoric *megaron*, a rectangular hall with columned porch which had been the nucleus of the Mycenaean palace. The earliest historical temples of which there are remains, of the 8th century B.C., are small versions of this *megaron* (see the illustration on page 86). Then architects surrounded the central hall (*cella*) with a complete colonnade, which was apparently made of wood; in the Age of Expansion in the 7th century, increasing wealth permitted the building of temples in stone. Originally this would have been a native limestone or other easily worked stone, which was plastered and painted brightly; but by the 5th century, marble was used at Athens and elsewhere.

Throughout the archaic period, columns were usually Doric, that is, they rested directly on the platform (*stylobate*) and had simple capitals. Above the row of capitals was a horizontal course (*entablature*) and then alternating *metopes* (square spaces which could be sculptured) and *triglyphs* (representations in stone of the ends of wooden cross-beams). In the Ionic style the columns were thinner, with bases and volute capitals. The third great style of column, the Corinthian, had a complicated capital copied from acanthus leaves; it was used mainly after 400 B.C. and has been very popular in modern times (as in Washington, D. C.).

The roof of a temple had a slight gable. Usually the rafters were wooden, covered by terracotta roof-tiles; rain spouts shaped like the heads of lions or other beasts were normally found along the long edges. In the two ends, pedimental sculptures could be placed; and on the rooftree there was room for other sculptures, often made of terracotta so that they would be light.

Although the temple form was essentially simple, subject to little major change, Greek architects continually made the proportions more refined and harmonious; today an archeologist who finds only a few scraps of the columns and entablature of a temple can often reconstruct precisely its shape and estimate its date fairly accurately. It is generally agreed that the most perfect example of the Greek temple is the Parthenon, which is pictured on page 73; another Greek temple of about the same time, at Paestum in Italy, is shown on page 139.

Architects also designed round buildings, both temples and secular structures; meeting halls for the council of a *polis;* marketplaces with covered porches and ornamental fountains; and walls. Private houses, however, had no architectural pretensions at this time, nor were there any public school buildings.

Sculptors worked hand in hand with the architects to decorate the temples. They also made reliefs to decorate altars and tombstones; above all they created statues to be placed near the temples and dedicated to the gods. Here again the basic forms had been set in the little figurines of the Dark Ages, but suddenly in the early 7th century, sculptors began to carve virtually life-size statues in marble. Bronze statues also were made in great numbers, but most were eventually melted down (one great surviving example is the Zeus shown on page 27).

One of the shapes most often used for statues was the young male, nude and in a standing position of repose. This figure, called the *kouros,* was recognizably a human being, but in the Archaic period the male body was not realistically depicted. The hands were held stiffly at the sides, the left leg was slightly advanced, the muscles of the chest were merely suggested, and the face and hair were stylized. Often the mouth was drawn up in a slight smile, the famous "Archaic smile." During the 6th century, sculptors moved toward realism in the sense that the bodies accorded more and more with what they saw every day in gymnasiums.

Just after 480 the last remains of Archaic stiffness yielded, and sculptors carved their statues in the Classic style. The parts of the body were closely interrelated, the old conventional pose of hands and legs was replaced by more relaxed and varied attitudes, the faces show a severe, self-assured spirit (as in the Apollo of Olympia shown on page 14). One of the great Classic sculptors was Phidias, who worked on the Parthenon at Athens. He also designed the great statue of Zeus at Olympia which was praised in later ages as "enhancing the majesty of the god." Another famous sculptor was Polyclitus of Argos, who presented his male figures ready to throw a spear or prepared for other action.

On the coast of Asia Minor sculptors usually clothed their male figures, and everywhere in Archaic and Classical times female figures were shown dressed. Sometimes they were seated on thrones and in

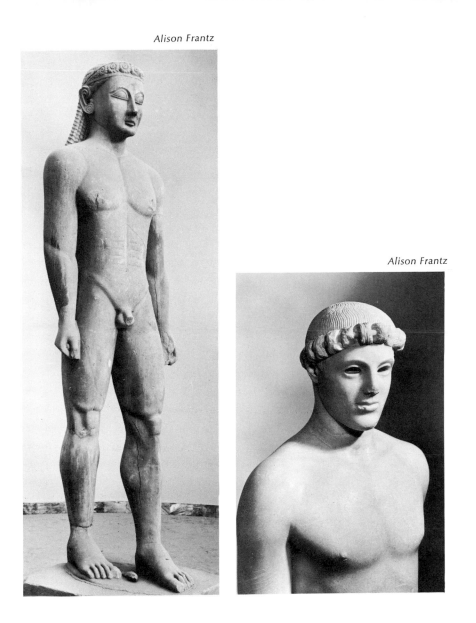

The Greek Male

These statues show the two boundaries of Archaic art. The youth from Cape Sunium, which was carved about 600, is over 9 feet high. He stands stiffly; his ears, hair, eyes, and chest look as they do because of the sculptor's effort to create an abstract harmony. The other statue was erected on the Acropolis just before 480. The hair is still stylized, but otherwise abstraction is yielding to a much more supple representation of the human body.

Friedrich Hewicker

The Greek Female

The female statue shown above, which was dedicated by Nikandre at Delos about 650 B.C., may be our oldest surviving large-scale Greek sculpture. Here the human form is just peeping out of the original marble block.

The two maidens on the next page are both from the Acropolis deposit. The one with the Archaic smile is the *peplos kore,* made about 540-530. Some of the original paint (red hair, irises, lips; black pupils, eyebrows, eyelashes) has survived. The other *kore* was dedicated a generation later, just before the Persian sack of the Acropolis. The severe, firm gaze sums up the spirit of 5th-century Athens.

these cases probably represented goddesses; very often female figures were standing (the *kore* type). One great collection of archaic *korai* comes from the Acropolis; discarded as old-fashioned after the Persian sack, they were used to fill up a hole on the top of the hill. As some of these ladies still show, the Greeks painted their sculptures to show the pattern of the textiles and to accentuate hair, lips, and other parts.

Beyond architecture and sculpture the same development from Archaic to Classical can be followed in many other arts. In pottery, as we have seen on earlier pages, the line of progress from the beginning of the Dark Ages down to the great achievements of the Athenian potters is clear and direct. In pottery too there was a great leap forward in the early 7th century, from Geometric to "Orientalizing" styles and then steady progress. In the 7th and early 6th centuries the decorated pottery of Corinth, Sparta, and other centers was popular; but by the mid-6th century the black-figured pottery of Athens was beginning to sweep the Mediterranean markets. From about 525 until 400 the red-figured pottery of Athens was dominant. Since the potters illustrated many aspects of daily life, they are an important historical source, and pictures of pottery have been used frequently in the preceding pages.

The Greeks also did large-scale painting, as we know from literary sources, but these works have all disappeared. So too most bronze work has been melted down, but in excavations at Olympia and other shrines archeologists have found tripods, armor, and other bronzes. Always, the Greeks designed their products—household furniture and other practically useful objects as well as coins and seal stones—to be beautiful.

Greek civilization, in sum, shows one of the world's great artistic spirits, on which all later ages have drawn for models and inspiration; still today a painter like Picasso often reflects in his work a deep knowledge of Greek art. Even little objects, such as bronze figurines or Athenian vases, can sell for tens of thousands of dollars and are the pride of any museum that acquires a fine specimen. Full-scale original statues are almost beyond price, and even Roman copies of Greek sculpture, which were made in abundance, have been eagerly sought since the days of the Renaissance popes and princes. But this is not just a modern craze; Greek artistic products were widely attractive in the ancient world from India on the east to Italy and central Europe on the west.

THE WESTERN GREEKS

Students of Greek history usually pay little attention to the great masses of Greeks who settled in "Greater Greece," southern Italy and eastern Sicily. These Greeks had little effect on the political history of the Aegean world, but they deserve notice for other reasons (see map on pages 106–7).

Culturally there was a constant interchange between the Greek homeland and the western states. Pythagoras and Xenophanes, two of the great 6th-century philosophers, moved to Italy and began a stream of philosophic thinking which eventually produced formal logic; Plato learned as much from the western philosophers as from his master Socrates. The study of rhetoric became an independent topic in education first at Syracuse and then was brought by Gorgias to Athens in the late 5th century, where the sophists perfected it. Frequently the tyrants of Sicilian cities won the chariot races at Olympia and Delphi and commissioned odes by Pindar or set up statues of their victorious chariots. Aeschylus himself died at Gela in Sicily, and Herodotus lived at Thurii in southern Italy for a while.

In the arts the western Greeks were very active. The revenues of their rich farmlands and commerce allowed them to build some of the largest temples ever constructed. Nowhere are more temples preserved side by side than at Paestum in Italy (Greek Posidonia) or Acragas and Selinus in Sicily. Native Sicilian states adopted Greek culture; one such state, Segesta, began a lovely temple high on its mountainside but it

Bank Leu

Nike (Victory) flies over a turning chariot, crowning it for an Olympic victory. Below is a crab, the symbol of Acragas.

A noble horseman of Gela, with raised lance.

was never finished. Temples were decorated with metopes and other works of sculpture, which sometimes are provincial in nature but at other times are as skillful as anything carved in Greece itself.

Politically too the history of the western Greeks is fascinating. Often they were under the control of tyrants, whose despotism became legendary. Phalaris, master of Acragas in Sicily, was said to have made a bronze bull in which he roasted his opponents; their cries bellowed out of the bull's mouth. Whether ruled by tyrants or by aristocrats, the Greek states of Sicily and Italy were able to beat off outside threats, like that of the Etruscans in Italy or the Carthaginians in Sicily; but they fought each other with equal enthusiasm. One of the greatest states in southern Italy, Sybaris, which was renowned for its luxury and gives us the word "sybarite," was wiped out by its neighbors about 510 B.C., and many states in Sicily suffered temporary destruction.

Generally the most important state was Syracuse, which led in the great repulse of the Carthaginian attack of 480 (the year of Salamis). At this time Syracuse was controlled by the magnificent tyrant Gelon; after his death Syracuse eventually became a democracy and withstood the great expedition by Athens in 415–413. Thereafter Syracuse again fell in the hands of a tyrant, Dionysius I, who wiped out most of his neighbors and built some of the greatest fortifications ever erected by Greeks. Dionysius was extremely suspicious of would-be assassins and was said to sleep in a room surrounded by a moat of water. After his death his realm eventually fell to pieces, and the Greek states resumed their fighting.

Temple of Poseidon, Paestum, one of the best preserved Greek temples

The end result of the constant wars was the same in the west as in the Aegean. Greece fell to Philip of Macedonia; the western Greeks found themselves less and less able to withstand native attacks and eventually came under the rule of Rome. In both cases the conquered civilized their conquerors (as the Roman poet Horace later put it). Philip's son Alexander was to carry Greek culture over the Near East; and the Romans expanded it over western Europe as far as Britain.

A mid-6th-century metope from an older temple at Paestum, recently discovered. It shows two girls fleeing desperately, chitons hiked up; since we do not have the companion piece we do not know who was chasing them. The design is reduced to its essentials.

6

The Decline of the Greek States
440-336 B.C.

The Peloponnesian War (**431–404 B.C.**) 🙂🙂🙂🙂🙂🙂🙂🙂🙂🙂🙂🙂🙂🙂🙂
The Athenian empire of the time of Cleon had three great results.
On the favorable side, it kept out the Persians, and it helped to make
Athens the economic and cultural center of the Greek world. But the
third result was a terrible catastrophe to the Greeks generally and to
the Athenians in particular.

Athenian aggressiveness frightened the conservative Spartans; the
historian Thucydides considered this the major underlying cause of
the war which broke out between Athens and Sparta. As a young
man he decided to write a history of the Peloponnesian war, and
since he was exiled for a mistake he made while he was a general he
had the leisure to observe the unpredictability and growing savagery
of the long conflict. His history is one of the greatest and most fright-
ful explorations of the nature of war. Thucydides also grimly chron-
icles the deterioration of the Athenians when an unexpected plague
killed one-third of their population (including Pericles) and the war
dragged on year after year.

Whereas Herodotus in the previous generation had ascribed the
Persian defeat in the end to the will of the gods, Thucydides allowed
no part to the gods in human development. History was the product
of men's calculations and passions, confounded by the accidents of
life; and so he wrote his great, concentrated study of the Pelopon-

nesian war "to last forever" and to be read by those "who want to understand clearly the events which happened in the past and which (human nature being what it is) will, at some time or other and in much the same ways, be repeated in the future."

Most historians today doubt that history repeats itself, but certainly they find the Peloponnesian war very illuminating. In the first place it was a struggle of a democracy against a more conservative form of government—and the Spartan system proved to have greater staying power and produced better leaders in the end. Also the Spartans had the moral support of the free Greek world against Athenian imperialism.

In the second place the war was a struggle of the elephant and the whale; for Sparta had a fine army but only a weak navy, and Athens had a small army but an excellent navy. The Spartans could invade Athens by land but could not force its army to come out and fight or make it surrender as long as it could be supplied by sea. The Athenians, on the other hand, could raid the coasts of Sparta by sea and try to tempt its helots to revolt, but they dared not meet the Spartan army in a battle.

The first phase of the war lasted from 431 to 421 and was fought very carefully by both sides. After a decade they agreed in exhaustion to a negotiated peace. The Athenians, who were discontented by so small a return for their sacrifices, next sought to extend their empire all the way to Sicily by conquering Syracuse, but their amphibious attack of 415–413 was one of the most complete catastrophes in history.

The war in the Aegean then resumed in its second phase, from 413 to 404. Because most of the Athenian subjects were embittered by Athenian exactions and had lost many of their men in the Syracusan expedition, they rebelled in 413. The Spartans felt they had a better chance of winning now and reopened the Peloponnesian war.

While the Athenians had been throwing away their strength on the foolish Syracusan expedition, the Spartans had been considering the reasons for their earlier lack of success. They realized they had to have a strong navy if they were to blockade Athens by land and sea alike—but a navy cost huge sums of money both for its construction and for the pay of its rowers. In desperation the Spartan leaders turned to the old foe Persia and made a devil's bargain to turn over the Greeks of Asia Minor to Persian rule in return for the necessary funds. The inexperienced Spartans lost their first fleet, but eventually the brilliant Spartan leader Lysander destroyed the Athenian fleet at Aegospotami in the Hellespont (the main route by which Russian wheat came down to Athens).

After enduring a siege for several months, the starving Athenians had to surrender in the spring of 404. Many of the Spartan allies wanted to destroy Athens forever, but the Spartans refused to go so far. Female oboe-players accompanied the enthusiastic levelers of the Long Walls and the walls of Piraeus, "deeming that day the beginning of liberty to Greece," and the Athenian navy was thereafter limited to 10 ships. For a brief while Athens itself gave up democracy and was ruled by the oligarchy of the 30 Tyrants, which was encouraged by Sparta.

The Collapse of Sparta (404–371) 🜂🜂🜂🜂🜂🜂🜂🜂🜂🜂🜂🜂🜂🜂🜂🜂🜂🜂🜂
Throughout their history the Spartans had limited their policy to repelling any external or internal danger to their security at home; but the great Athenian threat in the latter part of the 5th century now led them to make a fateful change. Staying home had never given them peace; so they decided to exercise direct power over all of Greece and prevent the rise of any league that could upset the peace.

Unfortunately the Spartans proved to be even more brutal masters than the Athenians had been. The Spartans found the chaos in Greece a source of unending difficulties. The long years of the Peloponnesian war had ruined many men, who became mercenaries for any state which could pay them; the Phocians even seized the oracle of Delphi, near their home, and melted down many of its treasures to pay their troops. In addition, the unrest made fiercer the old strife between rich and poor in every state.

For 30 years (404–371) the Spartans barely maintained their control. Many of the Spartan men were killed in the frequent wars; wealth and luxuries were brought home and corrupted Spartan simplicity; and finally in 371 the Spartan army was beaten in an open battle at Leuctra in Boeotia. For a decade (371–362) the victorious Thebans in turn tried to rule Greece but in vain. By 362 all the major Greek states were exhausted. Behind the scenes the Persians used their gold in bribes and largely determined what happened in Greece; the Greeks of Asia Minor were mostly under direct Persian rule.

Fourth-Century Art

The *Hermes* by Praxiteles is one of the very few surviving Greek original masterpieces by a famous artist. It was found at Olympia. Today it is set on a base within a large sandbox (in case there is an earthquake and it falls over). Originally Hermes held a bunch of grapes, for which the infant Dionysus is reaching. In its high polish, physical realism, and soft face the statue illustrates the great change from 5th-century severity.

Humor in Greek art is very rare, but this 4th-century vase from Boeotia seems to show a traveler who has dropped his knapsack and is running away from an ogress. Two other men are already up in a tree, having abandoned their plough beneath. The great days of Athenian vase-painting were over.

Fourth-Century Culture

Although the 4th century was a dismal period of foreign wars and internal revolutions, Greek civilization by no means ended. Some of the greatest Greek writers and artists lived in this period. The most vigorous men often came to Athens, whose economy had revived very quickly after its defeat and whose democratic system had been restored. Still, men could feel at home everywhere and as individuals were less bound by ties of patriotism than before.

The cultural change that took place during the 4th century is evident in every field. Gods who appealed to individual human beings, such as the healing god Asclepius, became much more popular (the theater of his shrine at Epidaurus is illustrated on page 78). Sculptors and other artists became more skillful technically but gave up the severe, dignified aspects of the Classic style for a more emotional appeal to individual sensitivities. Tragedies and poetry in general were not favored in this more commonplace world; the great writers were orators and philosophers.

In the last decades of the 5th century, Athens had been the scene of a great struggle between two generations. The older generation was deeply religious, strongly patriotic, and convinced that social life must be governed by ancestral virtues; the younger generation questioned everything and lived in part for its own pleasure. The thinkers who expressed the views of this younger generation were the sophists, who were, as we saw earlier, the first great educators beyond the elementary level.

Isocrates

The most important successor of the sophists in the 4th century was Isocrates, who lived to be 98 years old and wrote almost to the day he died. He was born before the Peloponnesian war began, and he died after the battle of Chaeronea, in which Philip of Macedonia became master of Greece. In his youth he listened to Socrates, then in the war lost his family estate and barely made a living until he gained a reputation as a teacher years later.

In his school Isocrates taught some of the greatest statesmen and generals of the 4th century. Like the sophists he emphasized rhetoric, but unlike his predecessors he insisted that education should show men how to lead a virtuous life in society. For him, the truly educated man was one who made the right decisions, not one who knew everything. No teacher ever did more than Isocrates to set the aims

Socrates (a Roman copy of a Greek bust which emphasized his bulb-nose and round head).

and methods of education. Isocrates also set Greek prose style. This in turn was the model first for Ciceronian Latin and then for modern English prose down through the 18th- and 19th-century classics.

Socrates and His Pupils 🖩🖩🖩🖩🖩🖩🖩🖩🖩🖩🖩🖩🖩🖩🖩🖩🖩🖩🖩🖩🖩
Among the greatest figures of the 4th century were two philosophers, Plato and Aristotle, who made great advances on lines marked out by Socrates. A great figure, Socrates spent his life questioning the standards of his fellow Athenians. He did not himself write any philosophical treatises, however, and we do not know very much about his own views.

The famous Socratic method consisted of probing a man's beliefs and showing their inconsistency so as to reduce the victim to an admission of his own ignorance, the first step toward true wisdom. The brilliance of his cross-examination with its paradoxes and swift analyses attracted many young nobles; it also deeply angered their elders, who associated the gadfly Socrates with the equally critical sophists.

Yet Socrates, unlike most of the sophists, was concerned primarily with ethical questions rather than teaching practical skills. Unlike earlier philosophers he found scientific problems of little interest; he learned far more from artisans and from medicine, the only science based on real experience and exact knowledge of man. As the famous Roman thinker Cicero later put it, Socrates brought philosophy down from the skies. The legacy of Socrates to 4th-century philosophers was a broad understanding of the issues involved in rational analysis and a sharp logical sense.

For years Socrates talked in the covered porches of the Agora, emphasizing the need for virtue to the materialistic, imperialistic Athenians of the late 5th century. Many of the young men who admired him were anti-democratic or even traitorous, and in 399 Socrates was tried on the grounds that he corrupted the youth and denied the gods of the Athenian state. The objective of this prosecution was in part simply to seek a scapegoat for the troubles of Athens after the collapse of 404, but Socrates' attackers also hoped to make him admit that the state had a right to dictate the opinions of an individual. Socrates refused, was condemned, and died as a martyr to the freedom of individual reason. Part of his defense is given in Part III.

The greatest pupil of Socrates, Plato, was disgusted by this result of democracy and left Athens for a while. Eventually Plato returned to open a research institute in the grove called the Academy just outside Athens. Here Aristotle, the son of a Greek doctor, came from northern Greece in 368 and studied for 20 years until the death of Plato. After a few years on the east coast of the Aegean, where Aristotle sharpened his ideas of politics and studied marine biology, he served as tutor of the young prince Alexander of Macedonia until the prince suddenly became king in 336 on the murder of his father Philip. Aristotle then opened his own research center and school at Athens, called the Lyceum, and spent the last 13 years of his life in feverish study of virtually all phases of human knowledge.

Comparison of Plato and Aristotle 🎇🎇🎇🎇🎇🎇🎇🎇🎇🎇🎇🎇🎇
Plato and Aristotle differed in many ways. Plato wrote dramatic dialogues in which his old teacher Socrates was presented as the leader of a group of thinkers searching for the nature of justice (the *Republic*) or love (the *Symposium*) or the origins of the world (the *Timaeus*). Few other philosophers in history have written so well and communicated to their readers the enthusiasm of the search for truth. Aristotle, on the other hand, was so busy that he had no time to polish his many treatises, which are outwardly dull, even incomplete at times.

Beside ethics and political theory Plato's main interests were mathematics and physics. While Aristotle studied everything, he was more attracted to biology, where he classified species in a system not improved until Linnaeus went to work in the 18th century and created the system we use today for flowers and animals. In all his scientific works Aristotle first collected and assessed all available information, then formed a general hypothesis, and finally tested his hypothesis against specific examples—the scientific method.

Plato always sought to discover the *theoretical* principles, such as the "ideas" of truth and the good, of which earthly instances were only incomplete examples. To put it in philosophical terms, his approach was idealistic and transcendental. Aristotle, on the other hand, was the founder of philosophical realism; he started from the *actual* world and felt that general principles or causes could be understood only as found in earthly reality. Plato's and Aristotle's works on political theory show their philosophical differences well:

Demosthenes
(Roman copy of an original which
was set up after his death)

Plato tried to construct a model of a perfect state in his *Republic*, and in his *Laws*, written much later, set up a state that was more like a modern totalitarian state than Athenian democracy; Aristotle's *Politics* on the other hand was primarily a practical study on how to eliminate civil war within the Greek states.

Both Plato and Aristotle were certainly men of the 4th century. In their political theory they thought solely in terms of the *polis*. Both inherited from Socrates a great concern for ethics and a sharp sense of logic; the logic one studies in school today, in fact, begins with Aristotelian logic. But both of them were really addressing their arguments to individual men, not to the state as a whole.

Each too has had a great and enduring influence in later ages. The "fathers" of the early Christian church borrowed heavily from Plato. Aristotle's logical and scientific works were almost unquestioned in the Middle Ages, and thinkers like Galileo and Newton had to fight hard against a general belief in his erroneous ideas on physics and mechanics. In his own work, however, Aristotle was the first great Greek scientist; his researches began the greatest century of scientific thought in history before modern times.

The Career of King Philip 〰〰〰〰〰〰〰〰〰〰〰〰〰〰〰〰

Throughout the earlier part of the 4th century, as the Greek states ground themselves to pieces, the Persian kings became almost as powerful in the Aegean as they had been before 480. Perhaps they should have gone on to invade Greece once more, but the memories of their failure in 480–479 made them cautious. The result was a power vacuum in mainland Greece, which was unexpectedly filled by the rise of Macedonia.

In 359 a wily, determined man, Philip, became king of Macedonia. At this point his realm was a large, but weak, kingdom just north of Greece, yet Philip immediately set about a career of unlimited expansion. He borrowed the Greeks' methods of training and organizing infantry, to go along with the fine cavalry provided by his Macedonian nobles. He also centralized the administration of his kingdom and established a number of cities. These were organized on Greek models, but unlike a *polis* they were firmly dependent on royal control.

First Philip conquered the barbarians on his northern and eastern frontiers; then he turned against Greece itself. By this time Athens, Sparta, and Thebes had all tried in vain to dominate the Greek world. All three were politically worn out but unwilling to cooperate with each other; many states were subject to civil strife between the rich and the poor. Philip skillfully exploited these divisions and used the gold and silver of Macedonian mines to bribe politicians.

As Philip rose higher and higher, however, he alarmed the greatest orator Athens ever produced, Demosthenes, and Demosthenes spent the period after 352 exhorting the Athenians in great speeches called "Philippics." The next 14 years were a duel. On the one side stood King Philip, sole master of his kingdom, with a good army of loyal Macedonians. On the other was the democratic leader Demosthenes, who had trouble persuading his fellow Athenians to use their money for military and naval preparations rather than for social security or in doing their own fighting instead of hiring mercenaries. At the end of the 14 years there came an open war, and Demosthenes reached the height of his career when he persuaded the Thebans to fight alongside the Athenians.

At the battle of Chaeronea, August 2, 338 B.C., however, only the Athenians and Thebans stood for Greek freedom. Although they fought hard all day, the victory fell to Philip's coordinated infantry and cavalry (the latter was led by his young son Alexander).

Time Chart No. 5: Greece, 440-336B.C.

B.C.	Major Events	Writers and Artists
440	**Athenian Mastery**	**Classic Art** Herodotus
431	Peloponnesian war: 1st phase	Sophocles sophists
421		Euripides Aristophanes
415	Athenian expedition to Syracuse	Thucydides
413	Peloponnesian war: 2nd phase	
404	**Spartan Mastery**	
399	Trial of Socrates	Isocrates
	Dionysius I (Syracuse)	Plato Xenophon
371	**Theban Mastery**	Praxiteles (*Hermes*)
362	**No Mastery**	
359	Philip king	Aristotle
	Rise of Macedonia Demosthenes (Athens)	
338	✂ Chaeronea **Macedonian Mastery**	
337	league of Corinth	
336	murder of Philip, Alexander king	

Philip treated Thebes roughly and put a garrison in its castle. To Athens, which still had the best navy in Greece, he was far more polite and offered an alliance, which the Athenians accepted. Then Philip assembled delegates from all the Greek states, except the stubborn Sparta, at the isthmus of Corinth and formed the league of Corinth in 337. Its published objectives were to stop the external and internal warfare which had plagued Greece and to protect the freedom of the seas; but it also had a joint army, commanded by Philip. For Philip planned next to attack Persia, and sent an advance force ahead to Asia Minor. In 336, however, he was murdered by a discontented Macedonian noble, and his son Alexander suddenly became king at the age of 20.

The Course of Greek History. Thus far we have followed the rise of Greek civilization from its dim beginnings in the Dark Ages. Next came the Age of Expansion. Then Greece became politically organized in little independent states, each jealous of its neighbor and ready to fight over the slightest cause; the victory of King Philip owed much to this division. Yet the *polis* encouraged a deep patriotism in its citizens, which is illustrated in the career of Demosthenes. Against Philip he lost, but he came very near winning.

The political history of Greece in the Age of Expansion and across the 5th and 4th centuries has many lessons for modern men. The scale of action was very small, and life at the time was much more simple than in industrialized societies; but for both these reasons some of the most enduring problems of interstate rivalry and internal conflict are perhaps easier to see.

Even more important to us, however, is the development of Greek civilization. In the arts, in literature, in philosophy, in medicine and science, the Greeks had already by 336 created masterpieces and models for later ages. The outward form of an epic like the *Iliad* or of a tragedy like *Oedipus the King* may seem strange to us at first glance, but the content soon produces a tremendous impact in a reader. Actually the Greeks themselves were already making their civilization more cosmopolitan, sophisticated, easier for foreigners to admire and imitate. The expansion of Greek civilization which followed is the next part of our story.

PART II

The Expansion of Greek Civilization

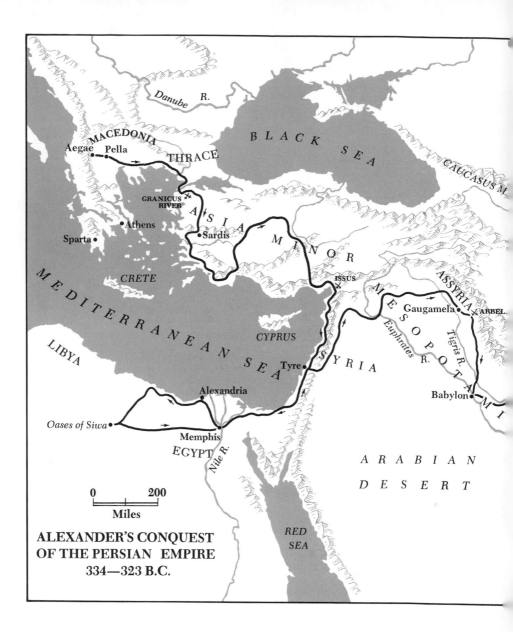

**ALEXANDER'S CONQUEST
OF THE PERSIAN EMPIRE
334—323 B.C.**

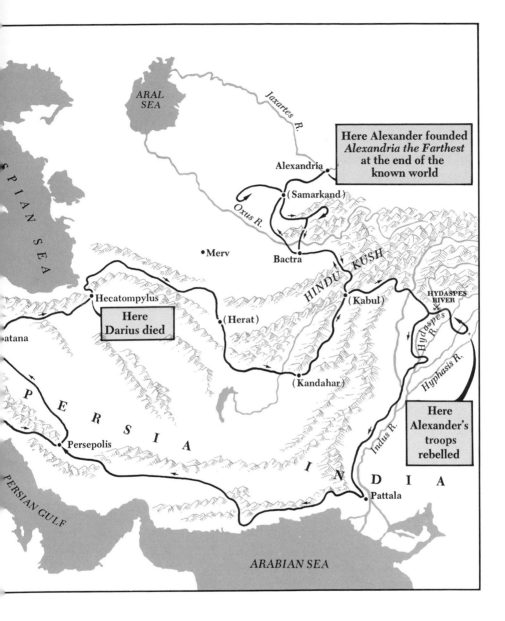

ARAL
SEA

Jaxartes R.

Here Alexander founded
Alexandria the Farthest
at the end of the
known world

Alexandria

(Samarkand)

Oxus R.

•Merv

Bactra

HINDU KUSH

CASPIAN SEA

Hecatompylus

Here
Darius died

(Herat)

(Kabul)

HYDASPES
RIVER

Hydaspes R.

Hyphasis R.

atana

(Kandahar)

P   E   R   S   I   A

I   N   D

Here
Alexander's
troops
rebelled

Persepolis

Indus R.

I   A

PERSIAN GULF

Pattala

ARABIAN SEA

The history of Greek civilization is usually divided into two parts. The first we have just looked at; this is called Greek history proper, or sometimes Hellenic history (from the word "Hellenes," which the Greeks used to describe themselves).

The second is rather different, for in it the Greeks spread their culture over the Near East. This later and wider period is nowadays termed the Hellenistic, or Greek-like, age. Between the Hellenic and the Hellenistic eras stands the great figure of Alexander of Macedonia, who conquered all the Persian empire in a blaze like a meteor.

The expansion of Hellenistic civilization is a fascinating story, which shows how attractive Greek arts and literature had become to other peoples. Christianity developed within this world; Saint Paul, for instance, knew a good deal of Hellenistic philosophy and literature. When the Romans became civilized, they largely imitated the Hellenistic model.

The later period of Greek civilization also had significant effects elsewhere, north into Russia and east into India. At the close of the story we shall look briefly at what was happening generally in Eurasia during the Hellenistic period, which can be dated from 323 to 30 B.C.

7

Alexander The Great

Alexander Becomes King 🔲🔲🔲🔲🔲🔲🔲🔲🔲🔲🔲🔲🔲🔲🔲🔲🔲🔲🔲🔲🔲

Alexander has conquered the imaginations of men over the centuries more than any other ancient political figure. From Albania to Afghanistan mothers have quieted their children with stories of the mighty warrior "Iskander"; a popular modern Greek folk tale warns sailors that if a mermaid comes up and threatens their ship they can ward it off by crying "Alexander is alive and rules." Yet his career covered just 13 years, 336–323 B.C., and he was dead at the age of 33.

Alexander was the son of King Philip of Macedonia and Queen Olympias, who was a fiery-tempered mother. In his youth he was tutored by the great philosopher Aristotle, who implanted in him a deep love of Greek culture; at the battle of Chaeronea he commanded the left flank at the age of 18. Then he and his mother fell at odds with Philip and withdrew from the court. When his father was murdered by a discontented noble in 336, Alexander became king of Macedonia and also master of Greece.

For the first two years of his reign Alexander had to put down the barbarians on his northern frontiers and quell a revolt of Thebes. To teach the Greeks not to rebel when his back was turned he destroyed all Thebes except for the house where the poet Pindar had once lived. Then he was ready to continue his father's plan, to invade Persian Asia Minor; but Alexander's dreams and his successes were to lead farther into the heart of Asia than Philip could ever have imagined. Throughout Alexander's marches two objects were placed under his pillow every night—a copy of Homer's *Iliad* (which Aristotle had corrected) and a dagger. These symbolize well his passionate yet heroic nature, which was never satisfied.

The Conquest of Persia

In the spring of 334 Alexander crossed the Hellespont with an army of 30,000 infantry and 5000 cavalry. This was small compared to ours in modern times, but it was as large a force as a general could supply from the countryside. In its discipline and tactics it was the mightiest fighting machine the Aegean had ever produced.

As Alexander advanced, reinforcements flowed from Macedonia to replace the losses. He was careful to keep his lines of communications open by leaving garrisons and some of his most able generals at key points. And always he knew what lay before him. Often he could encircle an enemy's position by a flank march over hidden trails even in areas he had never seen before. Geographers, scientists, and a historian accompanied the royal court on its 22,000-mile march, gathering information on areas which Greeks had not previously visited.

Immediately after crossing into Asia, Alexander moved to Troy. There he sacrificed to Achilles and took from a temple armor said to have belonged to the great Greek hero. Then he met the Persian satraps of Asia Minor in a battle at the Granicus river, in which the Persian objective was to kill him and so end the Macedonian threat. Alexander, white plumes on his helmet, boldly led his cavalry across the deep-banked river and, although slightly wounded in the battle, won the day. That night, weary as he must have been, he visited all his wounded soldiers; the corpses of the dead were sent back to Macedonia for great funerals. There has perhaps never been a greater general than Alexander in gaining the loyalty of his men as well as in taking just the right steps to win his battles.

For the next two years, 334–332, the most important problem facing Alexander was the fact that he had no navy but that the Persians did, which meant the Persians could possibly raise a revolt in Greece itself. To check this threat he had left his best general Antipater with a sizable army in Macedonia, but he also dealt directly with the naval problem by marching along the entire length of the Persian seacoast as far as Egypt, taking its ports as he went. The

One of the greatest mosaics found in ancient Pompeii was this scene of the battle of Issus. It probably is a copy of a famous painting made about 300 B.C. Alexander, bareheaded, charges at Darius, who is turning, on the point of flight. The figure of Alexander himself is shown on a larger scale below.

idea was simple, but no one since has managed to use land power to wipe out sea power in this fashion. To execute it required two great battles (Granicus and Issus), four major sieges, and many smaller engagements. In the 7-month siege of Tyre, Alexander's men had to build a mole from the coast out to the island of Tyre, mount siege towers on ships, and even fight under the water against Tyrian divers who tried to cut holes in the bottoms of the ships. But his soldiers stuck to their jobs and won.

Alexander met the Persian king Darius himself in battle, at Issus in 333, and defeated him decisively. Darius escaped; but his wife, who was pregnant, his mother, and his children were captured. To regain his family the Persian king sent an offer to Alexander of the western half of his realm plus a daughter in marriage. When Alexander read the letter to his council, his general Parmenio said that if he were Alexander he would accept. "So would I," replied Alexander, "if I were Parmenio," and rejected the compromise.

By 332 Alexander had entered and taken Egypt, the last Persian possession on the Mediterranean. Here two significant events occurred. First, Alexander made a detour to visit the great oracle of Zeus Ammon at the oasis of Siwa. The priests greeted him as the "son of Zeus," the first step toward his being made a living god as the successor of Near Eastern absolute rulers. The second event was his deliberate creation of a new city just west of the mouths of the Nile so that its harbor would not silt up. This was the first and greatest of the many Alexandrias he was to found and remains today one of the major cities of the Mediterranean world.

In 331 Alexander retraced his steps from Egypt to Syria and plunged inland to find Darius and defeat him in a decisive battle. At Issus, Darius had lost the Greek mercenaries who furnished his army with its stable infantry, and he was now unable to reach Greece to recruit replacements. This time the Persians had to rely mainly on their cavalry and a secret weapon, chariots equipped with scythes on their wheels which would roll through and slice up the Macedonian phalanx. The Persians also laid waste the route they expected Alexander to take and poisoned the wells, but, as always, Alexander learned what lay before him and he took another road. Near Arbela in upper Mesopotamia the two armies met; Alexander looked over the enemy carefully, gave his orders, and went to sleep so soundly that Parmenio had to wake him for the battle (October 1, 331).

Alexander was heavily outnumbered and stationed a reserve in his rear lest he be encircled—the first time in Greek warfare that we hear of the use of a reserve. The main battles took place between the cavalry on either flank. Alexander directed the action on his right wing while Parmenio had to hold the left flank as best he could with weaker forces. Darius, however, let his chariots advance too soon, so the Macedonian phalanx had room in which to spread out and let them dash harmlessly through.

All the while Alexander kept his eye on the ill-trained infantry in the Persian center, where Darius sat on a lofty throne on a wagon. At just the critical moment, when the Persian center was drawn apart toward the fierce battles on either flank, Alexander left his right-wing cavalry, hurried over to the phalanx, and led it in a triumphant charge straight through the middle at Darius. The Persian king fled, so did his center, and then his cavalry yielded the field on the two flanks.

After the victory Alexander marched to Babylon and gave his troops a month's leave in the greatest city of the Near East. Then he crossed the mountains into Persia proper and took the fortress-treasury of Persepolis, which he burned. Assertedly this was to punish the Persians for burning Athens 150 years earlier, but hostile tongues wagged that he and his companions had set it afire in a drunken brawl, encouraged by an Athenian harlot.

At the moment, treasure was not the most important thing to Alexander. He had to get his hands on Darius, who had fled toward the Caspian Sea. As Alexander chased relentlessly, he exhausted first his infantry, then most of his cavalry, but on he plunged. Darius' companions and generals panicked at the pursuit and killed Darius, leaving the body behind for Alexander. At this point, in May 330, Alexander could claim to be the legal master of the Persian empire.

Alexander in the East

The generals of the late Darius scattered defiantly into the eastern provinces (modern Turkestan and Afghanistan), where Alexander pursued them. The ensuing campaigns from 330 to 326 were the most difficult that he fought, and are for us the least illuminated. Since the Greeks knew little of this distant area in later days, geographical indications in the histories of Alexander are often imprecise. At times the mist lifts, and we see Alexander's men plodding over snow-covered passes 14,000 feet high, where they had to eat

The winter of 330 Alexander spent at Kabul (in modern Afghanistan). The next spring he crossed the Hindu Kush mountains north into Turkestan. To surprise his enemies he used the most difficult pass (the Khawak pass, 11,600 feet high, shown above).

raw mule to keep going. On another occasion native rebels defended themselves on a rock with sheer sides, but a picked Macedonian band surprised them by climbing the rear wall on pegs they had driven into the rock.

These eastern campaigns required different tactics, and Alexander was so great a general he could change to suit the terrain. Thus he divided his army into several independent columns in order to pin down semi-guerrilla opposition over wide areas. He also found it necessary to increase the percentage of horsemen and to re-equip his cavalry with native horses, which were very swift and enduring. Along the way, to safeguard his routes of communication, he settled bands of war-weary veterans in colonies. As time went on, these colonies throve and became centers of Greek civilization; some of them, such as Herat and Kandahar, are still major cities today.

Everywhere Alexander was successful in the end. In 327 his army marched down the Khyber pass and other routes into northern India, which had owed loyalty to the Persian king. On the Hydaspes river, a branch of the Indus river, he met the native rajah Porus, over 6 feet tall, who was equipped with war elephants. Alexander could not force a crossing of the wide river directly opposite Porus, but by constantly threatening to do so he weakened the enemy's attention. Finally, on a stormy night, he quietly led his men upstream, crossed undetected, and at daybreak was ready to give battle to Porus.

Since the Macedonian cavalry could not bring its horses close to the war elephants, the infantry had to win primarily on its own; as many Macedonians fell on this one day as in the battles of the Granicus, Issus, and Arbela combined. Porus himself was captured and brought before Alexander. When the latter asked Porus how he should be treated, Porus replied, "Like a king," and Alexander gave him back his realm as a subject king.

The geographers of the time had greatly underestimated the size of India and Alexander thought he could reach the end of the world if he drove his men eastward. On the river Hyphasis, in the heavy rains of the full monsoon, they finally rebelled and refused to go any farther. Alexander sulked in his tent for several days, hoping in vain they would beg him to come out and lead them; then he yielded and consented to turn back. But, being Alexander, he did not take the short road west; instead, he marched down the Indus river to the Persian gulf, conquering as he went, and then along the bleak coast of the gulf, where his men almost died for lack of food.

By 324 Alexander had returned as far as Susa. Some of the provincial governors he had appointed had proven incompetent and had to be replaced, and there was much other work of government to carry out. He reorganized the financial system of the empire by setting up large tax districts independent of the provinces and by minting the silver hoard of Persepolis on the Athenian standard of coinage. He and many of his officers took eastern wives, and he began training Persian youths to serve in the phalanx. When he dismissed many of his veteran Macedonians to go back home in retirement, they rebelled, but Alexander broke the revolt by arresting the ringleaders himself. Then he held a great feast of reconciliation at Opis, just outside Babylon, where he prayed to "the union of the Macedonians and Persians."

Alexander spent the winter of 324–323 laying plans to conquer Arabia to round out his realm and carousing with his friends. His constitution had been weakened during his eastern campaigns and, when he caught a type of swamp fever, could not throw it off. On June 10, 323, he died.

Time Chart No. 6: Alexander's Conquests

B.C.	Major Events
359	Philip king of Macedonia
356	Alexander born
	education by Aristotle
338	✗ Chaeronea
336	Alexander king
	conquest of Persian coast
334	✗ Granicus
333	✗ Issus
332	siege of Tyre, Egypt (Alexandria founded) *invasion of Mesopotamia*
331	✗ Arbela
330	destruction of Persepolis death of Darius
	conquest of Middle East
327	*invasion of India*
326	✗ Hydaspes river
324	return to Susa
323	death of Alexander

Alexander's Significance

No man in history is more absorbing to consider than Alexander. As far as his personality is concerned, modern scholars hold very different opinions. Some think of him as a romantic dreamer who wished to spread Greek culture over the Near East and to unite the East and the West. Opponents of this view point out that his colonies, even if they did help greatly to spread Greek culture in subsequent centuries, were primarily military posts, as were the forts at Chicago, Detroit, and elsewhere in the early history of the American Middle West. Also it must be remembered that although many of his men married Persians, no Macedonian and Greek women were brought out for Persian men to marry.

Others call him a passionate military adventurer whose only delight was in fighting battle after battle like a Napoleon. This view

An idealized portrait of Alexander, in elephant headdress, which was struck in Egypt soon after his death.

stresses also the truth that his only real way of relaxing was to drink. In one drunken rage he killed his best friend Clitus, and many other supporters fell victim to his suspicions (even Parmenio was executed on fear of a plot). Still, Alexander did enter Asia as king of a great realm, and along the way he did engage, if spasmodically, in rather far-reaching reforms. Some scholars visualize Alexander as a very calculating, cold-hearted politician-general, as if he were a man of the 20th century. This view too is a distortion—one of the greatest problems in history is to avoid using modern standards by which to judge people of past ages.

Even more debatable is the question, did Alexander shape the history of the world? Many historians believe that great men alter the course of history; one well-known English scholar (Arnold Toynbee) has written of Alexander, "Had he not died young, he might have politically united the world. Today, instead of two war-ring camps, we might have had a united world, with no nuclear sword of Damocles over our heads." Few thinkers would agree with so extreme a statement, but many would argue that Alexander him-self was responsible for a new world, the Hellenistic age, in which the Greeks ruled the Near East for 3 centuries politically and almost 1000 years culturally.

Yet is it really true that one man could do so much? Greek civi-lization was already expanding vigorously over the Mediterranean; and many men had gone to the Persian empire as mercenaries, doctors, and traders for years before Alexander became king. Economic and social tensions within the Aegean had also produced a host of men ready to pour out into the Near East once a road was opened. In sum, did Alexander ride the crest of a wave which would have swept eastward anyway? Or did he himself have an important role in directing and shaping the course of events? These are the questions. Each student of history must furnish his own answers.

CHAPTER 8

The Hellenistic Age

Political Organization (323–30 B.C.) 🮣🮣🮣🮣🮣🮣🮣🮣🮣🮣🮣🮣🮣🮣🮣🮣🮣🮣🮣🮣
Alexander left no heirs of his own family of any importance. Shortly
after his death his widow Roxane gave birth to a son who never had
a chance to succeed politically because Alexander's army contained
very able, self-willed generals. Within two decades all the Macedonian royal house had been killed, and the marshals of Alexander
had carved up his huge realm into a number of independent kingdoms. There was incessant fighting, but no one general was able to
gain mastery over all the others.

Each Hellenistic kingdom included as much territory as an individual warlord was able to get and keep. One cautious general,
Ptolemy, seized the relatively isolated corner of Egypt and established the longest-lived line of kings. The Ptolemies of later years
also ruled southern Syria and parts of Asia Minor at times, and even
Greece occasionally. The last of the Ptolemies, Cleopatra, used her
charms first on Caesar, then on Mark Antony. She committed suicide
in 30 B.C. when the Romans finally conquered Egypt.

Another of Alexander's generals, Seleucus, grabbed the center of
the empire, from Asia Minor to India; but the kernel of the Seleucid
realm over the next two centuries was Asia Minor, Syria, and Mesopotamia. A third major kingdom was centered on Macedonia, which
usually contented itself with the control of neighboring Greece. This

Hellenistic Kings

Seleucus, in a helmet covered by a panther skin. He was the longest lived of Alexander's generals.

Demetrius (of the Antigonid family) won a great naval victory. Here Victory blows her trumpet on the prow of a warship.

kingdom came under the control of the Antigonid family. A number of smaller principalities existed in Asia Minor and other areas, and such Greek states as Rhodes and Byzantium maintained their independence.

Politically the Hellenistic world thus consisted of a number of not very well defined states which fought each other repeatedly to gain territory or to maintain a balance of power. The Seleucids and Ptolemies engaged in at least six "Syrian" wars over the control of south Syria and Palestine. This international rivalry led to embassies, dynastic marriages, and treaties of alliance or neutrality which resemble those of modern diplomacy. In the end each power weakened the other to such an extent that outsiders came in and swallowed them up piecemeal. By 30 B.C. the Romans had conquered all the Mediterranean shores, and an Iranian state called Parthia held the inland districts, including Mesopotamia.

Social Conditions

In some ways the Hellenistic world must remind one of the European expansion into Asia and Africa during the 18th and 19th centuries. That is, the Hellenistic kingdoms controlled great areas of the Near East and ruled them for their own profit, not for the benefit of the

Hirmer Fotoarchiv, München

Pergamum, in northwest Asia Minor, was the home of an independent king-dom. Its rulers adorned its citadel with magnificent buildings. This is one of the steepest theaters in the Greek world.

subjects. To maintain his control a Hellenistic king had to rely upon his army and also on a bureaucracy, and for both he recruited mainly Greeks and Macedonians.

The result was an outpouring of Greeks into the Near East, where they became the dominant social element over huge masses of natives. Greek was so much the language of administration, of law, of coinage that the natives almost disappeared from view. Yet they were actually the farmers and producers of the wealth enjoyed by the Greek upper class.

The Seleucid kings continued the policy which Alexander had begun and founded Greek cities over a large area. Asia Minor and Syria came to appear entirely Greek; the greatest cities there were Antioch in Syria and Seleucia in Mesopotamia (near old Babylon, which dwindled away). In Egypt the Ptolemies made little effort to create Greek cities, but Alexandria, their capital, was the greatest single cultural and economic center of the eastern Mediterranean.

Throughout all the Hellenistic cities, which stretched as far as Bactria, the style of administration and the architectural equipment of temples, gymnasiums, and other buildings were Greek, although the mass of inhabitants was native (as in modern Hong Kong or Singapore). Everywhere the drive and vigor of Greek civilization quickened the pace of life and brought many areas of the Near East and Middle East to a level of economic activity they had never before experienced.

Still, in the end the Hellenistic world was a system which in modern terms we would call "colonial," where the native population worked for the benefit of an alien few. In Egypt particularly we can see both how Greek efficiency first increased the productivity of the land and also how the peasants became growingly discontented at their exploitation. By the late 3d century B.C. they had begun to engage in sabotage and on occasion to murder Greek overseers; in the next century there were outright revolts. At this time too the Jews of Palestine, led by the Maccabee brothers, rebelled against Seleucid control (167 B.C. on). The Hellenistic kingdoms, in short, were weakened both by their international rivalries and by internal discontents; but socially the Greeks managed to maintain their dominance for centuries after the time of Christ.

Hellenistic Literature and Scholarship

The political and social developments after Alexander had a great effect on the ancient world itself. Achievements in the arts, literature, and science were in a sense even more important, for they have influenced Western civilization ever since—more directly than has any other phase of Greek culture.

The most appealing among the many authors of the period is undoubtedly Menander, who wrote over 100 comedies at Athens. These comedies were not like those of Aristophanes a century earlier, which had attacked political figures; Menander's stories largely revolve about lovers. Parents in Menander do not understand their children, who have to plot to get their own way. Cunning slaves, prostitutes, and other figures who cross the stage suggest the breaking down of old social standards. Menander showed good and bad with sympathetic understanding and quick wit; he is the source of many famous lines, such as "Whom the gods love die young." Even Saint Paul quotes him: "Evil companionships corrupt good morals."

The sands of Egypt still produce ancient papyri. A few years ago the play of Menander, *Dyskolos* (Bad-Tempered Man), turned up. To the right of the decorative symbol in the last column you can read, in larger print, Menandrou and Dyskolos.

In the Hellenistic age poetry revived after the lull in the 4th century. Some poets wrote learned epics; others turned remedies for snakebites into verse, celebrated the pleasures of the countryside, or composed witty epigrams. This poetry is often called "Alexandrian" inasmuch as it was centered on that city; in general it is marked by learned mythological references and a high polish. Frequently the meaning of the poets is as deliberately obscure as in modern verse. Milton drew heavily on Alexandrian styles, as have others down to the present day.

The poetry of earlier times had been designed for presentation to groups; Hellenistic verse was largely intended to be *read* by individuals. This was true of the abundant prose too. Romantic accounts of Alexander flourished alongside tales of imaginary heroes and heroines. Scientific and philosophic treatises were turned out by the hundreds. Particularly notable were the learned commentaries on

In the Hellenistic world many entertainers traveled about from city to city, giving plays or burlesque skits or performing the latest music. This band of street musicians is in a mosaic from Pompeii, which was made by Dioscorides of Samos.

Homer and other earlier authors, along with critical editions of the great Greek authors and studies in grammar. These works, mostly written at Alexandria from the 3d century B.C. on, began a tradition of scholarly criticism on which Christian thinkers later leaned very heavily in studying the Bible. This tradition survived across the Middle Ages and served as a model for modern historical study and literary criticism.

Hellenistic Science

The field in which Hellenistic civilization broke the freshest ground was that of science. Aristotle had established the scientific approach in the time of Alexander, and across the next few generations there came the greatest explosion of scientific interest the world saw before the 16th century after Christ. This interest was centered in

Alexandria, where the Ptolemies supported the creation of the greatest library of the ancient world as well as a research institute called the Museum.

In medicine Herophilus was the first to study anatomy by dissecting corpses. He traced much of the nervous system, and his contemporary Erasistratus did the same for the veins and arteries. Erasistratus came close to discovering the theory of the circulation of the blood, which William Harvey was not to propose until the 16th century. In the biological field on the whole, however, the most important practical advances came in the improvement of plants and animals for farming purposes through the deliberate selection of better specimens.

Developments in the physical sciences and in mathematics were even more notable. The astronomer Aristarchus advanced the guess that the earth revolved around the sun, but he postulated movement of the planets on circular orbits at regular speeds. This theory conflicts with observable evidence, and as the greatest astronomer of ancient times (Hipparchus) said, "We must abide by the facts of observation." So Hipparchus and others perfected a mathematical scheme of the heavenly system which put the earth at the center of the universe but came closer to agreeing with the known evidence. In the 16th century Copernicus ran across a reference to Aristarchus and was led to his own theories.

Hipparchus also invented trigonometry, partly in order to improve geographical measurements. The Greeks not only knew that the earth was round but had a method of measuring its size; they were only 200 miles off from the correct figure. The most-lasting single achievement of Hellenistic mathematics, though, was the composition of the most famous textbook ever written, in which Euclid summed up and systematized earlier Greek geometrical reasoning. The more original mathematician Archimedes of Syracuse became a legendary hero for devising skillful machines to withstand the Roman siege of his native town in 212 B.C.

The Weaknesses of Ancient Science

Despite his own practical work Archimedes said he "looked upon the work of an engineer and everything that ministers to the needs of life as ignoble and vulgar." This expresses one defect of Hellenistic science: it was not intended to lead to practically useful results. Another problem was the limited range of ancient technology. Hero of

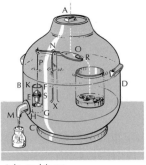

Adapted from
Hero, Pneumatics, fig. 21

The First Vending Machine
If a coin is inserted through opening A at the top, it will fall on plate R and depress it. The other end rises and elevates rod P so that holy water will flow out through opening M. The coin falls off plate R after it is depressed; some coins can be seen at the bottom of the container. The drawing is a modern reconstruction from the text of Hero's description.

Alexandria made a simple steam engine, but this and other inventions could not be put into general use because iron-workers could not provide adequate materials. Further, observations were hampered by the lack of instruments: there were no microscopes, thermometers, or even accurate yardsticks.

Perhaps most important of all as a check to scientific study was the generally held view that the natural world, no less than mankind, was fundamentally alive and was divinely governed. To understand its character one could better turn to philosophy and to religion than to science, which was little more than a hobby. In the disasters of life, prayer or resignation to the will of God were the principal props for man. Before the end of the Hellenistic period scientific advances had almost stopped; but the achievements of the scientists down to this time had created the picture of the world and man which Western scholars accepted until Copernicus, Galileo, and Harvey.

Hellenistic Philosophers 🙾🙾🙾🙾🙾🙾🙾🙾🙾🙾🙾🙾🙾🙾🙾🙾🙾🙾🙾🙾🙾🙾🙾
The writings of Hellenistic philosophers were as dry as those of the scientists. Most of them have disappeared, but the ideas they proposed have had tremendous effects ever since they were written. Essentially these philosophers were seeking to give guidance to individual men so they could live with serenity in an unstable world.

Two schools of thought came down from the past. Plato's Academy continued to flourish, but it had now become a conservative center for men who felt it was impossible to reach ultimate decisions. An Academic of the Hellenistic world simply balanced possible alternatives and skeptically did whatever seemed best at the moment. Aristotle's Lyceum also survived, largely as a focus for scholarly and literary activity. Out of these schools and the work of other early Greek philosophers, however, more vigorous approaches emerged.

One was that of the Cynics, who disdained the conventions of the day and urged that men live simply and in accordance with the ways of nature. The Cynic Diogenes was said to have spent most of his time in a tub; when Alexander the Great came to visit him and asked if he wanted anything, Diogenes replied, "Yes, please don't block my sunshine." Cynics often gave "sermons" or short, practical speeches to the men in the streets and harbors of the Hellenistic cities.

Another school of thought was that founded by Epicurus, who was a contemporary of Menander at Athens. Epicurus took over the atomic theory of Democritus and used it to demonstrate that the gods had no effect in the world; man's soul was an accidental grouping of atoms which dissolved on his death. So the Epicurean objective was to enjoy *this* life with the least amount of pain, and virtue was meaningless except if it might aid that enjoyment. Epicureans accordingly gained a bad name as atheists and pleasure-seekers, but in strict Epicurean theory a man would lead a very simple, secluded life so as to avoid pain and distress. Falling in love and having children were two sure ways to such distress. No other ancient philosophy was as rationally derived from a few simple premises as Epicureanism.

More generally influential was the Stoic philosophy, which eventually became the principal philosophy of Greece and then of Rome. Saint Paul learned about Stoicism in his home town of Tarsus. This philosophy was begun by a gaunt merchant from Cyprus named Zeno, who came to Athens on business just before 300. In Athens, Zeno became interested in the problems which philosophers debated and remained there for the rest of his life, arguing with them in short, clipped paradoxes in the Stoa of the Athenian marketplace. Later Stoics developed and altered his terse opinions, so Stoicism cannot be summed up as easily as the sharp, clear doctrine advanced by Epicurus.

In general, however, the Stoics created a view based on the theory of the 5th-century thinker Heraclitus that the supreme power or Zeus was divine reason or fire (*logos*), a spark of which resided in each human being. The world was directed by a rational plan, and it was the duty of each man to live so as to improve his soul (divine spark) and to understand the divine will which governed all. What happened to his body was incidental (hence our meaning of "stoic"); his mind was free and must accept the cardinal virtues of temperance, judgment, bravery, and justice. Moreover, all men were basically equal brethren, living in the great city which we call the world, under the rule of Zeus.

Stoicism and Christianity

In its practical advice Stoicism was markedly like Christianity, but the theories behind the advice were quite different. Stoics eventually accepted astrology as revealing the divine will; they had, moreover, no concept that a human being had an individual eternal existence. When a man died, his divine spark or soul went back into the divine "logos." Some Stoics argued indeed that at the end of a very long era the whole world "burned up" and started over on exactly the same course; thousands of years from now, in this theory, we shall all be here again, doing exactly the same things.

Most people found it very hard in practice to live up to another part of Stoic theory. This was the doctrine that one must eliminate all emotional responses lest they affect one's internal tranquility. An ideal wise man was pitiless though he would work unflinchingly for his fellow men and do his duty by family and state. As Christian preachers later pointed out, true Christians on the other hand must love their neighbors; and as was observed, Christ Himself had emotions.

The Greek Character of the Hellenistic Age

During the Hellenistic age Greeks lived all over the Near East. Sometimes they were scattered as administrators in Ptolemaic Egypt; sometimes they were grouped as the governing circles of the major cities. Everywhere, however, they clung to their Greek inheritance just as English tea-planters or civil servants upheld British customs throughout Asia and Africa in the 19th century. There was no real fusion of the Greek and the Near Eastern cultures.

Partly the Greeks maintained their ways by establishing shrines of Greek gods, but primarily they did it by giving their children a Greek education. Since Greek was the language of government and the foreign culture was very appealing to the more well-to-do natives, considerable parts of Near Eastern society also sought to gain the same kind of education. By the close of the Hellenistic period, as a result, even those Jews who lived outside Palestine had to have the books of Moses (Old Testament) translated into Greek so they could use them.

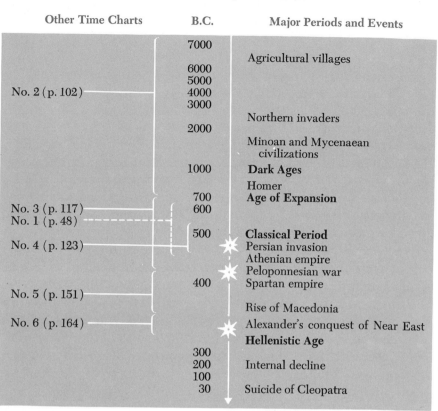

Time Chart No. 7: Greece, 7000 to 30 B.C.

Other Time Charts	B.C.	Major Periods and Events
	7000	
		Agricultural villages
	6000	
	5000	
No. 2 (p. 102)	4000	
	3000	
		Northern invaders
	2000	
		Minoan and Mycenaean civilizations
	1000	**Dark Ages**
		Homer
	700	**Age of Expansion**
No. 3 (p. 117)	600	
No. 1 (p. 48)		
	500	**Classical Period**
No. 4 (p. 123)		Persian invasion
		Athenian empire
		Peloponnesian war
	400	Spartan empire
No. 5 (p. 151)		Rise of Macedonia
No. 6 (p. 164)		Alexander's conquest of Near East
		Hellenistic Age
	300	
	200	Internal decline
	100	
	30	Suicide of Cleopatra

The Spread of Greek Civilization.   Three centuries stretch from the death of Alexander to the suicide of Cleopatra, which marks the end of political independence for the Hellenistic world. In these centuries Greek civilization spread outside the Aegean widely and deeply; the only possible comparison in history is the expansion of Western civilization after Columbus and the other explorers.

The thinkers and artists who lived in ancient Greece were relatively few in number, and their framework of life was very simple. Yet their achievements were amazingly varied and influential. All of us who read these pages are using an alphabet which the Greeks evolved and passed on to the Romans; and the ideas in our heads about many important aspects of life are framed the way they are because the ancient Greeks once lived. Greek civilization, in short, was the first great phase of Western civilization.

Town Planning

Hellenistic Art

**Eurasia
in the
Hellenistic Age**

TOWN PLANNING

Alexander is said to have founded 70 new cities. Although this figure is certainly an exaggeration, one of his successors, Seleucus, created at least 59. Many of these setlements had roots in earlier native communities, but all were reclothed in Greek dress politically and architecturally.

The old cities of Greece had largely grown up in a haphazard form. Even in Hellenistic times Athens was described as "very dry, because the supply of water is poor; as a result of its great age it is not divided into regular blocks. Most of the houses are poor, only a few stand out somewhat. At first sight visiting strangers will scarcely believe that this is the famous city of the Athenians."

The colonies in Sicily and Italy, however, had often been laid out in a more regular fashion. In the late 5th century B.C. the port of Athens itself, the Piraeus, had been redesigned to have straight streets crossing at right angles, by the famous town-planner Hippodamus of Miletus; sections of the Piraeus were consciously assigned to the various functions of a port. So Alexander and his successors had a fund of practical and theoretical knowledge on which to draw when they founded Alexandria, Antioch, Seleucia, and other major and minor cities of the Hellenistic world.

In general the streets were straight and formed rectangular blocks, but often were adjusted to the slope of the terrain. Each block usually

Priene was an average-size city in Asia Minor, on the slope of a mountain across the bay from Miletus. This reconstruction is based on its excavation early in the 20th century.

Within the walls the streets are laid out on rectangular lines. The *agora* is in the center, surrounded by porches; to its upper left is the temple of Athena, and straight up the hill is the theater. The large structure at the bottom is the gymnasium, with a stadium to its right.

included several houses, which often had common external walls and extended forward to the narrow sidewalks. The rooms in a house were normally placed about a courtyard; mosaic floor decoration was common at least in better homes. The well-to-do in Hellenistic times lived far better than had Cleon and his wife in 440 B.C.

Close to the center of the city lay an *agora* or marketplace, decorated with covered porches and public buildings. Other areas were set aside for temples, a gymnasium, and theater. Harbor towns had sales halls and warehouses as well as breakwaters to protect the busy ship-

Looking across the Agora to the Stoa of Attalus, built in Hellenistic times and rebuilt recently by the American School of Classical Studies. Beyond is the Acropolis, crowned on this side by the Erechtheum.

ping; special war harbors existed at Alexandria, Carthage, and elsewhere. At Alexandria the great lighthouse or *Pharos* was erected, and another of the famous Seven Wonders of the world, the huge statue or Colossus of Rhodes, stood near the port of Rhodes until the great earthquake of 222 B.C.

The architectural styles of the Hellenistic world were derived from those of Classic times, but builders emphasized size and decoration. The ornate Corinthian capital, for instance, became much more common than the simple Doric column. Round buildings were also erected in greater numbers, but major innovations in building materials and styles had to wait until the Roman empire. Fortifications, however, reached an advanced stage; most cities were very carefully walled.

HELLENISTIC ART

If most of us were asked to name a great Greek sculpture the answer would probably be "Venus de Milo." This statue was found on the island of Melos about 150 years ago and was secured by the French after an international competition so violent that it resembles a spy-story. It was probably carved in the 2d century B.C.; its polish and technical skill well illustrate the main characteristics of Hellenistic art. The statue is also Hellenistic in that Aphrodite (as we should call her) is for the most part unclothed; Archaic and Classical ladies were almost always dressed. Earlier sculptors had worked in a style very different from the Hellenistic.

The qualities which marked Hellenistic sculpture had begun to appear in the 4th century (before the time of Alexander) but were spread widely over the Mediterranean thereafter. Sculptors had mastered external grace and supple movement and coupled these often with an emotional, romantic approach. In depicting historic characters Hellenistic artists were far more realistic than in Classic times; this realism could even become brutal in representations of battered boxers or old men and women. Complicated groups which were set up at Pergamum and Athens to represent the defeat of the invading Gauls show a remarkable violence and twisting of the human figure (see the example on page 188).

Hellenistic sculpture was much liked by the Romans. Since it was

Venus de Milo

Fototeca Unione

A decorative painting on stone, showing girls at play with knuckle bones (the ancient dice). This painting was found at a site near Pompeii but was probably painted by a Greek.

either taken to Rome as booty or copied there in abundance, men in western Europe appreciated Greek art largely through these examples of Hellenistic style from the Renaissance until the last century, when Archaic and Classic art became better known.

Artistic products of the Hellenistic age were not limited to large pieces of sculpture for display in marketplaces and temples. Painting was very popular, and it is unfortunate that only a few paintings have survived. Mosaic-workers first used native pebbles to make designs but

A pair of gold earings
in the shape of dolphins

A gold bracelet in the form of
two snakes, with a garnet
at the center

then carefully arranged specially prepared stones; sometimes the subjects of mosaics were drawn from famous paintings, as in the Alexander mosaic on page 159. Bronze- and silver-workers made candelabra, vases, and other handsome objects. Particularly noticeable was the great increase in the amount of gold jewelry which was made from Hellenistic times onward; earlier Greeks had not been prosperous enough to be able to afford necklaces, earrings, and bracelets of gold in such abundance.

Even after Alexander ordinary men could not buy work in gold or erect large statues, but they could purchase less expensive objects as substitutes. Blown glass was developed in the Hellenistic period and was used widely for goblets and vases. Cheaper metals could be worked into jewelry which "looked like the real thing." Terracotta figurines of animals or gods and goddesses had long been dedicated in temples or graves, but in Hellenistic times common citizens bought such figurines for decorative as well as religious purposes. Sometimes the subject was taken from popular plays; ladies with fans, hats, and other accessories were turned out by the thousands. One figurine shows two women playing oboes from a camel in a religious procession, another brutally pictures a slave being flogged; these small, mass-produced wares are a lively reflection of contemporary life.

Probably the one site which best shows us all the aspects of Hellenistic art is not in the Hellenistic world at all. This is the city of Pompeii in Italy, which was buried by an eruption of Mount Vesuvius in A.D. 79. Pompeii was a Roman town, but its arts and crafts owed much to Hellenistic skills in every field; several of the pictures on the preceding pages are from Pompeii and the area around it. Other examples, however, turn up all the way to Afghanistan and India, a fact that indicates Hellenistic products were attractive to people everywhere.

Schmuckmuseum, Pforzheim Langlotz,
Die Kunst der Westgriechen, fig. 159

Two dancers
from Tarentum

EURASIA IN THE HELLENISTIC AGE

So far we have talked about the rise of Greek civilization and then its spread over the Near East. Anyone who follows this story might think that the Aegean world and Near East were cut off by a wall from the rest of Eurasia; but this obviously was not true. In actual fact Greek culture had had some influence outside its Aegean home since the beginning of Greek colonization in about 750 B.C.; particularly after Alexander this influence increased markedly. In turn, alien cultures came slowly to affect the Greek way of life.

The progress of all these other parts of Eurasia is a long history which cannot be taken up here in detail; but any curious student of a period always likes to know, "What's happening elsewhere?" The two areas of which one thinks first are undoubtedly India and China; both were creating very different forms of civilization in the days when Western civilization was first beginning in Greece.

India. The vast peninsula of India had always been more open to the west than China was. Men could make their way by sea up and down the Persian gulf; sometimes they traveled overland to the Indus river. People who called themselves Aryan and spoke a language distantly connected to Greek (Sanskrit) had entered India at some point after 2000 B.C. In Greece invaders of this wave ended the Mycenaean world; in India the Aryans toppled a declining civilization focused on the Indus river which had used writing and had built huge cities. The ballast for one modern railroad line came from the bricks piled up in one of these cities.

Thereafter, in the centuries just on either side of 1000 B.C., the Indians seem to have established that combination of caste system and village organization which has survived ever since. The Hindu religious outlook which goes along with this social organization, however, was not fully consolidated until after the time of Christ.

When the Assyrian and Persian empires pacified the areas northwest of India, local kingdoms arose in the Indus and Ganges river basins. These took over the use of iron, of writing in an alphabetic script, of coinage, and of much else. In one of these kingdoms in about 500 B.C. the great practical preacher Gautama (the Buddha) provided an ethical guide to life which evolved into Buddhism.

Alexander's conquest of the northern fringe of India had great effects. Externally it opened the way for fairly continuous contacts with the Hellenistic world; internally it disturbed the structure of little kingdoms and led to the union of much of northern India into one realm. The greatest king of this state, Asoka, lived in the mid-3d century B.C. Asoka conquered central India, then became a devoted Buddhist in revolt against the bloodshed of his conquest. He sent missionaries of his faith to Syria and Egypt and set up inscriptions all over India in Greek and other languages in praise of the Buddha. Thereafter Greeks from Bactria moved down into northern India and ruled it in smaller states until the time of Christ; the coinage of these rulers often has Greek on one side and the native Indian script on the other.

From this time on, Indians began to build more lasting architectural works, such as temples. By the time of Christ they also showed the Buddha in human form. One influential group of artists in northwest India (the Gandhara school) adapted Hellenistic models, especially of Apollo, for this purpose; so the great, serene figures of the Buddha which exist all over Asia today go back mainly to a Greek source. The basic way of life in India was not altered by its Hellenistic contacts, but local development was sharpened and quickened by this link.

China. China was remote from the Near East; at least 2000 miles of inhospitable land lay between the two. China became civilized even later than India did; the first civilization took place on the Yellow river (in north China) and could not have been much earlier than 2000 B.C. Once Chinese civilization had appeared, though, it developed more continuously than has any other down to the present.

During the time when Greece was in its Age of Expansion, north

Outsiders in the Mediterranean World
In the 3d century, barbarous Gauls invaded the Aegean from the north. They were stopped in Asia Minor by the kings of Pergamum, who set up great monuments to commemorate the victory. This is a Roman copy of the central group in one monument: a defeated Gaul stabs himself after killing his wife. The emotion, twisting of the human body, and technical skill are characteristic of Hellenistic art.

China was ruled by the Chou line of kings, who were not able to maintain order or unity. About 500 B.C. the great thinker Confucius advanced his ideas that society must hold to its past, that both state and family must be based on moral principles, and that rulers must set examples for their people. In his practical, earthly approach Confucius has often been compared to the Greek philosophers, especially to Socrates. But Socrates is mainly a noble example of martyrdom for free reason, whereas the principles of Confucius were eventually accepted by Chinese civilization as its guide to life.

By Hellenistic times north China had been unified politically under the Han dynasty, which lasted from 207 B.C. to A.D. 220. Chinese power reached into southern China and Indochina, into Korea, and even across central Asia to the Near East for a short time about 100 B.C. In general, however, Chinese connections with the Hellenistic world were through intermediary caravan traders and involved little more than the sale of luxuries on either side.

The Rest of the Old World. China and India are only two small parts of the Old World. Throughout most of this vast expanse men and women lived and died across the generations with little perceptible change. Indeed, one large part, Africa south of the Sahara and upper Egypt, had little more contact in this period with the Mediterranean world than did the Americas, where the Mayan and Inca civilizations were beginning.

In the north of Europe and Asia great steppes reached from China to central Europe. Here nomads occasionally raided down into the civilized areas, but from about 600 B.C. to past A.D. 300—almost 1000 years —these raids were usually of limited nature. Modern Russian archeologists have uncovered in recent years burials of the nomad princes and other evidence which shows some acquaintance with civilized art styles, especially in metal work. In one case they discovered the elaborately tattooed body of a ruler; the body had been frozen in ice in a mountain burial.

If non-Western civilizations should become dominant over all the world at some future date, then students of ancient history will probably spend most of their time on the development of India or China, but those of us who share Western civilization today must first look back to the Greeks. From our point of view, the most important direction in which Greek civilization expanded was westward along the Mediterranean. The people there proved very receptive to Greek art and thought.

Chief among these turned out, in the end, to be the Romans, who rose from a little territory on the lower Tiber river in Italy and ruled all the Mediterranean world and many parts of continental Europe for centuries. Thanks to the Roman empire the basic qualities of Greek civilization, clothed in a Latin and Christian dress, became firmly implanted in western Europe.

From the south a few Negroes came down the
Nile to the Mediterranean. This figurine, which
was found at Priene (see page 179), shows a
Negro taking a thorn from his foot.

PART III

Sources on Athenian Democracy and Imperialism

SOURCES ON ATHENIAN

DEMOCRACY AND IMPERIALISM

Men of all ages have disagreed with each other violently on major issues, just as there are great problems today which divide us. Sometimes these disagreements of the past have only historical significance, for we are no longer interested in the subject of debate. At other times the arguments were over problems which are still important in modern life, and a study of them can afford us a fresh point of view.

The following pages give some of the major sources on two great issues in 5th-century Athens: the good and bad sides of democracy, in theory and in practice, and the nature of imperialism. Both are topics of importance today, but try to form your own judgment of Athenian democracy and imperialism without bringing in modern views. It will not be easy, but the effort will show how a historian proceeds.

1. Praise of Democracy

(Thucydides, *History*, Book II, sections 35–46, translated by Rex Warner)

When Athens was at war, its citizens solemnly commemorated those killed in action each autumn, after the fighting season was over. One part of the ceremony was a funeral oration by a leading statesman.

Alison Frantz

Another honor for those Athenians who died in war was the setting up of a stone slab with their names. This is a fragment of one year's list.

Usually the speaker linked the valor of those who died for their fatherland during the year with the earlier achievements of Athens.

In the autumn of 430 Pericles was selected to deliver the funeral oration at the end of the first year of the Peloponnesian war. Thucydides gives us Pericles' speech, which is the greatest surviving praise of Athenian democracy.

Unfortunately we cannot be sure that the speech contains only Pericles' ideas, for Thucydides stated in his introduction that he himself composed the speeches which occur in his story. Still, he goes on to say, "I endeavored, as nearly as I could, to give the general line of what was actually said," and he probably heard Pericles give the speech. So we must hope that the following views were in fact those of the leader of Athenian democracy.

The Funeral Oration deserves to be read twice: once to appreciate the merits of democracy, as Pericles describes them; and once to see if you can detect any criticisms of democracy which he is trying to oppose.

> Our system of government does not copy the institutions of our neighbours. It is more the case of our being a model to others, than of our imitating anyone else. Our constitution is called a democracy

because power is in the hands not of a minority but of the whole people. When it is a question of settling private disputes, everyone is equal before the law; when it is a question of putting one person before another in positions of public responsibility, what counts is not membership of a particular class, but the actual ability which the man possesses. No one, so long as he has it in him to be of service to the state, is kept in political obscurity because of poverty.

Just as our political life is free and open, so is our day-to-day life in our relations with each other. We do not get into a state with our next-door neighbour if he enjoys himself in his own way, nor do we give him the kind of black looks which, though they do no real harm, still do hurt people's feelings. We are free and tolerant in our private lives; but in public affairs we keep to the law. This is because it commands our deep respect.

We give our obedience to those whom we put in positions of authority, and we obey the laws themselves, especially those which are for the protection of the oppressed, and those unwritten laws which it is an acknowledged shame to break.

And here is another point. When our work is over, we are in a position to enjoy all kinds of recreation for our spirits. There are various kinds of contests and sacrifices regularly throughout the year; in our own homes we find a beauty and a good taste which delight us every day and which drive away our cares. Then the greatness of our city brings it about that all the good things from all over the world flow in to us, so that to us it seems just as natural to enjoy foreign goods as our own local products.

Then there is a great difference between us and our opponents, in our attitude towards military security. Here are some examples: Our city is open to the world, and we have no periodical deportations in order to prevent people observing or finding out secrets which might be of military advantage to the enemy. This is because we rely, not on secret weapons, but on our real courage and loyalty. There is a difference, too, in our educational systems. The Spartans, from their earliest boyhood, are submitted to the most laborious training in courage; we pass our lives without all these restrictions, and yet are just as ready to face the same dangers as they are.

Here is a proof of this: When the Spartans invade our land, they do not come by themselves, but bring all their allies with them; whereas we, when we launch an attack abroad, do the job by ourselves, and, though fighting on foreign soil, do not often fail to defeat opponents who are fighting for their own hearths and homes. As a matter of fact none of our enemies has ever yet been confronted with our total strength, because we have to divide our attention between our navy and the many missions on which our troops are sent on land. Yet, if our enemies engage a detachment of our forces and defeat it, they give themselves credit for having thrown back our entire army; or, if they lose, they claim that they were beaten by us in full strength.

Our love of what is beautiful does not lead to extravagance; our love of the things of the mind does not make us soft. We regard wealth as something to be properly used, rather than as something to boast about. As for poverty, no one need be ashamed to admit it: the real shame is in not taking practical measures to escape from it. Here each individual is interested not only in his own affairs but in the affairs of the state as well: even those who are mostly occupied with their own business are extremely well-informed on general politics—this is a peculiarity of ours: we do not say that a man who takes no interest in politics is a man who minds his own business; we say that he has no business here at all.

Taking everything together then, I declare that our city is an education to Greece, and I declare that in my opinion each single one of our citizens, in all the manifold aspects of life, is able to show himself the rightful lord and owner of his own person, and do this, moreover, with exceptional grace and exceptional versatility. And to show that this is no empty boasting for the present occasion, but real tangible fact, you have only to consider the power which our city possesses and which has been won by those very qualities which I have mentioned.

Mighty indeed are the marks and monuments of our empire which we have left. Future ages will wonder at us, as the present age wonders at us now. We do not need the praises of a Homer, or of anyone else whose words may delight us for the moment, but whose estimation of facts will fall short of what is really true. For our adventurous spirit has forced an entry into every sea and into every land; and everywhere we have left behind us everlasting memorials of good done to our friends or suffering inflicted on our enemies. This, then, is the kind of city for which these men, who could not bear the thought of losing her, nobly fought and nobly died.

You should fix your eyes every day on the greatness of Athens as she really is, and should fall in love with her. When you realize her greatness, then reflect that what made her great was men with a spirit of adventure, men who knew their duty, men who were ashamed to fall below a certain standard. If they ever failed in an enterprise, they made up their minds that at any rate the city should not find their courage lacking to her, and they gave to her the best contribution that they could. They gave her their lives, to her and to all of us, and for their own selves they won praises that never grow old. Famous men have the whole earth as their memorial: it is not only the inscriptions on their graves in their own country that mark them out; no, in foreign lands also, not in any visible form but in people's hearts, their memory abides and grows. It is for you to try to be like them. Make up your minds that happiness depends on being free, and freedom depends on being courageous.

As for those of you here who are sons or brothers of the dead, I can see a hard struggle in front of you. Everyone always speaks well of the dead, and, even if you rise to the greatest heights of heroism, it will be a hard thing for you to get the reputation of having come near, let alone equalled, their standard. When one is alive, one is always liable to the jealousy of one's competitors, but when one is out of the way, the honour one receives is sincere and unchallenged.

Perhaps I should say a word or two on the duties of women to those among you who are now widowed. I can say all I have to say in a short word of advice. Your great glory is not to be inferior to what God has made you, and the greatest glory of a woman is to be least talked about by men, whether they are praising you or criticizing you. I have now, as the law demanded, said what I had to say. For the time being our offerings to the dead have been made, and for the future their children will be supported at the public expense by the city, until they come of age. This is the crown and prize which she offers, both to the dead and to their children, for the ordeals which they have faced. Where the rewards of valour are the greatest, there you will find also the best and bravest spirits among the people. And now, when you have mourned for your dear ones, you must depart.

2. Criticism of Democracy
(Old Oligarch, *Constitution of the Athenians*, translated by H. G. Dakyns)

Pericles' remarks to the Athenian widows which you have just read are certainly not very comforting. They do not represent altogether the way women actually were treated in Athens. In his view of democracy, did he also stress theoretical virtues rather than reflect practical realities? As it happens, we also have a bitter pamphlet against the defects of Athenian democracy, written within the next few years by an anonymous critic. He is called the Old Oligarch.

Since this critic uses irony, his meaning is not evident at first glance. Basically he is against the idea of democracy, as he states at the beginning. Then he proceeds to show that, *if* Athens is to be a

democratic state, it has organized its government very well! The aim
of this argument is to prove to conservatives that the actual conduct
of public affairs—free speech and the choice of rascals, for example—
was as bad as the theory of democracy.

Frequently, as a result, he directly disagrees with Pericles. For
example Pericles says that in Athens "the claim of excellence is also
recognized"; the Old Oligarch asserts of the people, "the good folk
they are disposed to hate." You can find other illustrations of this
direct opposition.

Now, as for the constitution of the Athenians, and the type of
manner of constitution which they have chosen, I praise it not, in so
far as the very choice involves the welfare of the baser folk as opposed to that of the better class. I repeat, I withhold my praise so far;
but, given the fact that this is the type agreed upon, I propose to show
that they set about its preservation in the right way.

In the first place, I maintain, it is only just that the poorer classes
and the common people of Athens should be better off than the men
of birth and wealth, seeing that it is the people who man the fleet,
and have brought the city her power. The steersman, the boatswain,
the lieutenant, the look-out-man at the prow, the shipwright—these
are the people who supply the city with power far rather than her
heavy infantry and men of birth and quality. This being the case, it
seems only just that offices of state should be thrown open to every
one both in the ballot and the show of hands, and that the right of
speech should belong to any one who likes, without restriction.

In the next place, in regard to what some people are puzzled to
explain—the fact that everywhere greater consideration is shown to
the base, to poor people and to common folk, than to persons of good
quality,—so far from being a matter of surprise, this, as can be shown,
is the keystone of the preservation of the democracy. It is these poor
people, this common folk, this worse element, whose prosperity, combined with the growth of their numbers, enhances the democracy.
Whereas, a shifting of fortune to the advantage of the wealthy and
the better classes implies the establishment on the part of the commons of a strong power in opposition to itself. In fact, all the world
over, the cream of society is in opposition to the democracy. Naturally, since the smallest amount of intemperance and injustice, together with the highest scrupulousness in the pursuit of excellence,
is to be found in the ranks of the better class, while within the ranks
of the People will be found the greatest amount of ignorance, dis-
orderliness, rascality,—poverty acting as a stronger incentive to base

conduct, not to speak of lack of education and ignorance, traceable to the lack of means which afflicts the average of mankind.

The objection may be raised that it was a mistake to allow the universal right of speech and a seat in council. These should have been reserved for the cleverest, the flower of the community. But here, again, it will be found that they are acting with wise deliberation in granting to even the baser sort the right of speech, for supposing only the better people might speak, or sit in council, blessings would fall to the lot of those like themselves, but to the commons the reverse of blessings. Whereas now, any one who likes, any base fellow, may get up and discover something to the advantage of himself and his equals.

What it comes to, therefore, is that a state founded upon such institutions will not be the best state; but, given a democracy, these are the right means to secure its preservation. The People, it must be borne in mind, does not demand that the city should be well governed and itself a slave. It desires to be free and to be master.

As to bad legislation it does not concern itself about that. In fact, what you believe to be bad legislation is the very source of the People's strength and freedom. But if you seek for good legislation, in the first place you will see the cleverest members of the community laying down the laws for the rest. And in the next place, the better class will curb and chastise the lower orders; the better class will deliberate in behalf of the state, and not suffer crack-brained fellows to sit in council, or to speak or vote in the assemblies. No doubt; but under the weight of such blessings the People will in a very short time be reduced to slavery.

Another point is the extraordinary amount of license granted to slaves and resident aliens at Athens, where a blow is illegal, and a slave will not step aside to let you pass him in the street. I will explain the reason of this peculiar custom. Supposing it were legal for a slave to be beaten by a free citizen, or for a resident alien or freedman to be beaten by a citizen, it would frequently happen that an Athenian might be mistaken for a slave or an alien and receive a beating; since the Athenian People is not better clothed than the slave or alien, nor in personal appearance is there any superiority.

Or if the fact itself that slaves in Athens are allowed to indulge in luxury, and indeed in some cases to live magnificently, be found astonishing, this too, it can be shown, is done of set purpose. Where you have a naval power dependent upon wealth we must perforce be slaves to our slaves, in order that we may get in our slave-rents, and let the real slave go free. It is for this reason then that we have established an equality between our slaves and free men; and again

Laws, treaties, and even financial records were cut in stone and set up publicly in 5th-century Athens (which had no newspapers to publish important documents). This is a decree of the Assembly in 405 B.C. honoring Samos (shown above are the goddess Hera of Samos and Athena of Athens, clasping hands). It begins with the name of the secretary of the Council of 500 (Cephisophon), goes on to name other officials, and at the end of line 6 gives the proposer of the decree (Clisophus).

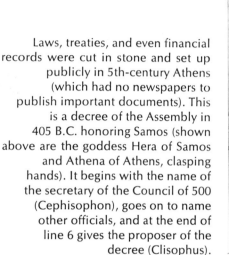

between our resident aliens and full citizens, because the city stands in need of her resident aliens to meet the requirements of such a multiplicity of arts and for the purposes of her navy. That is, I repeat, the justification of the equality conferred upon our resident aliens.

The common people put a stop to citizens devoting their time to athletics and to the cultivation of music, disbelieving in the beauty of such training, and recognizing the fact that these are things the cultivation of which is beyond its power.

States oligarchically governed are forced to ratify their alliances and solemn oaths, and if they fail to abide by their contracts, the offence, by whomsoever committed, lies nominally at the door of the oligarchs who entered upon the contract. But in the case of engagements entered into by a democracy it is open to the People to throw the blame on the single individual who spoke in favor of some measure, or put it to the vote, and to maintain to the rest of the world, "I was not present, nor do I approve of the terms of the agreement." Inquiries are made in a full meeting of the People, and should any of these things be disapproved of, they can at once discover countless excuses to avoid doing whatever they do not wish.

And if any mischief should spring out of any resolutions which the People has passed in council, the People can readily shift the blame from its own shoulders. "A handful of oligarchs acting against the interests of the People have ruined us." But if any good result ensue, they, the People, at once take the credit of that to themselves.

In the same spirit it is not allowed to caricature on the comic stage or otherwise libel the People, because they do not care to hear themselves ill spoken of. But if any one has a desire to satirize his neighbor he has full leave to do so. And this because they are well aware that, as a general rule, the person caricatured does not belong to the People, or the masses. He is more likely to be some wealthy or well-born person, or man of means and influence. In fact, but few poor people and of the popular stamp incur the comic lash, or if they do they have brought it on themselves by excessive love of meddling or some covetous self-seeking at the expense of the People, so that no particular annoyance is felt at seeing such folk satirized.

The People of Athens has no difficulty in recognizing which of its citizens are of the better sort and which the opposite. And so recognizing those who are serviceable and advantageous to itself, even though they be base, the People loves them; but the good folk they are disposed to hate.

For my part I pardon the People its own democracy, as, indeed, it is pardonable in any one to do good to himself. But the man who, not being himself one of the People, prefers to live in a state democratically governed rather than in an oligarchical state may be said to smooth his own path towards iniquity. He knows that a bad man has a better chance of slipping through the fingers of justice in a democratic than in an oligarchical state.

I repeat that my position concerning the constitution of the Athenians is this: the type of constitution is not to my taste, but given that a democratic form of government has been agreed upon, they do seem to me to go the right way to preserve the democracy by the adoption of the particular type which I have set forth.

3. The Place of Pericles

a. The Judgment of Thucydides

(Thucydides, Book II, section 65, translated by Rex Warner)

Thucydides was a ruthless critic of most political leaders, but he admired Pericles deeply. The historian summed up Pericles' abilities as follows:

After his death his foresight with regard to the war became even more evident. For Pericles had said that Athens would be victorious if she bided her time and took care of her navy, if she avoided trying to add to the empire during the course of the war, and if she did nothing to risk the safety of the city itself. But his successors did the exact opposite, and in other matters which apparently had no connexion with the war private ambition and private profit led to policies which were bad both for the Athenians themselves and for their allies. Such policies, when successful, only brought credit and advantage to individuals, and when they failed, the whole war potential of the state was impaired.

The reason for this was that Pericles, because of his position, his intelligence, and his known integrity, could respect the liberty of the people and at the same time hold them in check. It was he who led them, rather than they who led him, and, since he never sought power from any wrong motive, he was under no necessity of flattering them: in fact he was so highly respected that he was able to speak angrily to them and to contradict them. Certainly when he saw that they were going too far in a mood of over-confidence, he would bring back to them a sense of their dangers; and when they were discouraged for no good reason he would restore their confidence.

So, in what was nominally a democracy, power was really in the hands of the first citizen. But his successors, who were more on a level with each other and each of whom aimed at occupying the first place, adopted methods of demagogy which resulted in their losing control over the actual conduct of affairs. Such a policy, in a great city with an empire to govern, naturally led to a number of mistakes, amongst which was the Sicilian expedition. In the end it was only because they had destroyed themselves by their own internal strife that finally they were forced to surrender.

b. The Account of Plutarch
(Plutarch, *Life of Pericles*, translated by J. and W. Langhorne)

The Greek biographer Plutarch lived about A.D. 46–120, five centuries after Pericles. He too admired the leader of Athenian democracy, but also reported the criticisms which had been advanced.

Thucydides represents the administration of Pericles as favoring aristocracy, and tells us that though the government was called democratic it was really in the hands of one who had appropriated the whole authority. Many other writers likewise inform us that by Pericles the people were first accorded allotments of public lands, were treated at public expense with theatrical diversions, and were paid for the most common services. This new indulgence from the government was a bad custom which rendered the people expensive and luxurious and destroyed the frugality and love of labor which supported them before.

The chief delight of the Athenians and the wonder of strangers, which alone serves for a proof that the boasted power and wealth of old Greece is not an idle tale, was the magnificence of the temples and public buildings. Yet no action of Pericles moved the anger of his enemies more than this.

In their accusations to him to the people, they insisted that he had brought the greatest disgrace upon the Athenians by removing the public treasures of Greece from Delos and taking them into the Athenians' own keeping; that Greece must consider it an act of open tyranny when she saw the money she had been obliged to contribute toward the war lavished by the Athenians in gilding their city and ornamenting it with statues and temples that cost a thousand talents, as a proud and vain woman decks herself out with jewels.

Pericles answered this charge by observing that they were not obliged to give the allies any account of the sums they had received, since they had kept the Persians at a distance and effectively defended the allies. He declared that as the state was provided with all the necessities of war, its extra wealth should be laid out on works which would be eternal monuments of its glory, and which, during their execution, would bring universal abundance [by the pay to the workmen].

[After winning in this argument, about 443] Pericles became a different man; he was no longer so submissive to the humor of the populace, which is as wild and changeable as the winds. Pericles kept the public good in his eye and pursued the straight path of honor, for the most part gently leading the people by argument to a sense of what was right and sometimes forcing them to comply with what was for their own advantage.

Nor were the powers of eloquence alone sufficient, but as Thucydides observes the orator was a man of unblemished reputation. Money could not bribe him. Although he added greatly to the wealth of the state, yet he added not one drachma to his inherited estate.

4. Life and Death of Some Athenian Citizens

(Plato, *Apology of Socrates*, translated by Benjamin Jowett)

Most Athenian citizens, like Cleon, lived and died without entering into the pages of history. Some men were encouraged by the vigor of 5th-century Athens to create great buildings, statues, and plays. Others, however, suffered unpopularity, exile, or even death.

The most famous punishment of an unpopular man came in the trial of Socrates in 399. His accusers charged him with corrupting the young men of Athens (some of his disciples had led the right-wing revolution of the 30 Tyrants in 404) and denying the gods of the state, but the real ground of attack was his refusal to bow to popular opinions.

Plato later wrote the *Apology of Socrates,* which appears to be the speech Socrates delivered to the jury. Much of it probably comes from Plato's imagination; but the basic argument probably is due to Socrates. In the passage below, Socrates deals with the real ground of attack and defies the public. Partly as a result he was condemned and had to commit suicide by drinking poison.

> If you say to me, Socrates, this time we will not mind your accuser, and you shall be let off, but upon one condition, that you are not to enquire and speculate in this way any more, and that if you are caught doing so again you shall die;—if this was the condition on which you let me go, I should reply: Men of Athens, I honor and love you; but I shall obey God rather than you, and while I have life and strength I shall never cease from the practice and teaching of philosophy, exhorting any one whom I meet and saying to him after my manner: You, my friend,—a citizen of the great and mighty and wise city of Athens,—are you not ashamed of heaping up the greatest amount of money and honor and reputation, and caring so little about wisdom and truth and the greatest improvement of the soul, which you never regard or heed at all?
>
> For I do nothing but go about persuading you all, old and young alike, not to take thought for your persons or your properties, but first and chiefly to care about the greatest improvement of the soul. I tell you that virtue is not given by money, but that from virtue comes money and every other good of man, public as well as private. This is my teaching, and if this is the doctrine which corrupts the youth, I am a mischievous person. But if any one says that this is not my teaching, he is speaking an untruth. Wherefore, O men of Athens, I say to you, do as my accuser bids or not as he bids, and either acquit me or not; but whichever you do, understand that I shall never alter my ways, not even if I have to die many times.

Do you think that Socrates was intelligent to make this statement, when he was on trial for his life?

5. Athenian Imperialism

(Thucydides, Book V, sections 85–113, translated by Rex Warner)

In 416 the Athenians attacked the island of Melos (where the famous Venus was erected much later). The Melians protested that they had not opposed the Athenians and should be allowed to remain neutral. Thucydides inserted into his history a debate between the spokesmen of the Athenians and of the Melians. It is generally agreed that he made up this debate in order to show clearly the nature of imperialism.

Athenians: We on our side will use no fine phrases saying, for example, that we have a right to our empire because we defeated the Persians, or that we have come against you now because of the injuries you have done us—a great mass of words that nobody would believe. And we ask you on your side not to imagine that you will influence us by saying that you, though a colony of Sparta, have not joined Sparta in the war, or that you have never done us any harm. Instead we recommend that you should try to get what it is possible for you to get, taking into consideration what we both really do think; since you know as well as we do that, when these matters are discussed by practical people, the standard of justice depends on the equality of power to compel and that in fact the strong do what they have the power to do and the weak accept what they have to accept.

Melians: Then in our view (since you force us to leave justice out of account and to confine ourselves to self-interest)—in our view it is at any rate useful that you should not destroy a principle that is to the general good of all men—namely, that in the case of all who fall into danger there should be such a thing as fair play and just dealing, and that such people should be allowed to use and to profit by arguments that fall short of a mathematical accuracy. And this is a principle which affects you as much as anybody, since your own fall would be visited by the most terrible vengeance and would be an example to the world.

Athenians: As for us, even assuming that our empire does come to an end, we are not despondent about what would happen next. One is not so much frightened of being conquered by a power which rules over others, as Sparta does (not that we are concerned with Sparta now), as of what would happen if a ruling power is attacked and defeated by its own subjects. So far as this point is concerned, you can leave it to us to face the risks involved. What we shall do now is to show you that it is for the good of our own empire that we are here and that it is for the preservation of your city that we shall say what we are going to say. We do not want any trouble in bringing you into

our empire, and we want you to be spared for the good both of yourselves and of ourselves.

Melians: And how could it be just as good for us to be the slaves
as for you to be the masters?

Athenians: You, by giving in, would save yourselves from disaster;
we, by not destroying you, would be able to profit from you.

Melians: So you would not agree to our being neutral, friends instead of enemies, but allies of neither side?

Athenians: No, because it is not so much your hostility that injures
us; it is rather the case that, if we were on friendly terms with you,
our subjects would regard that as a sign of weakness in us, whereas
your hatred is evidence of our power.

Melians: We know that in war fortune sometimes makes the odds
more level than could be expected from the difference in numbers of
the two sides. And if we surrender, then all our hope is lost at once,
whereas, so long as we remain in action, there is still a hope that we
may yet stand upright.

Athenians: Hope, that comforter in danger! If one already has solid
advantages to fall back upon, one can indulge in hope. It may do
harm, but will not destroy one. But hope is by nature an expensive
commodity, and those who are risking their all on one cast find out
what it means only when they are already ruined; it never fails them
in the period when such a knowledge would enable them to take precautions. Do not let this happen to you, you who are weak and whose
fate depends on a single movement of the scale. And do not be like
those people who, as so commonly happens, miss the chance of saving
themselves in a human and practical way, and, when every clear and
distinct hope has left them in their adversity, turn to what is blind
and vague, to prophecies and oracles and such things which by encouraging hope lead men to ruin.

Melians: It is difficult, and you may be sure that we know it, for us
to oppose your power and fortune, unless the terms be equal. Never-
theless we trust that the gods will give us fortune as good as yours,
because we are standing for what is right against what is wrong; and
as for what we lack in power, we trust that it will be made up for by
our alliance with the Spartans, who are bound, if for no other reason,
then for honour's sake, and because we are their kinsmen, to come to
our help. Our confidence, therefore, is not so entirely irrational as you
think.

Athenians: So far as the favour of the gods is concerned, we think
we have as much right to that as you have. Our aims and our actions
are perfectly consistent with the beliefs men hold about the gods and
with the principles which govern their own conduct. Our opinion of

the gods and our knowledge of men lead us to conclude that it is a general and necessary law of nature to rule wherever one can. This is not a law that we made ourselves, nor were we the first to act upon it when it was made. We found it already in existence, and we shall leave it to exist for ever among those who come after us. We are merely acting in accordance with it, and we know that you or anybody else with the same power as ours would be acting in precisely the same way. And therefore, so far as the gods are concerned, we see no good reason why we should fear to be at a disadvantage. But with regard to your views about Sparta and your confidence that she, out of a sense of honour, will come to your aid, we must say that we congratulate you on your simplicity but do not envy you your folly. In matters that concern themselves or their own constitution the Spartans are quite remarkably good; as for their relations with others, that is a long story, but it can be expressed shortly and clearly by saying that of all people we know the Spartans are most conspicuous for believing that what they like doing is honourable and what suits their interests is just. And this kind of attitude is not going to be of much help to you in your absurd quest for safety at the moment.

When the Melians refused to give in, the Athenians surrounded them by a wall and eventually forced their surrender. As Thucydides briefly reports, "the Athenians put to death all the men of military age whom they took, and sold the women and children as slaves."

6. Athenians and Spartans
   (Thucydides, Book I, sections 70–71, 84, translated by Rex Warner)

At the end of the previous source there was disagreement between the Melians and Athenians about the character of the Spartans. This is worth looking at a little further; frequently the historian learns much from contrasts. The first passage below is a direct comparison of Athenians and Spartans, made by Corinthian ambassadors at Sparta just before the Peloponnesian war broke out.

You have never yet tried to imagine what sort of people these Athenians are against whom you will have to fight—how much, indeed how completely different from you. An Athenian is always an innovator, quick to form a resolution and quick at carrying it out. You, on the other hand, are good at keeping things as they are; you never originate an idea, and your action tends to stop short of its aim. Then again, Athenian daring will outrun its own resources; they will take risks against their better judgement, and still, in the midst of danger, remain confident. But your nature is always to do less than you could have done, to mistrust your own judgement, however sound it may be, and to assume that dangers will last for ever. Think of this, too: while you are hanging back, they never hesitate; while you stay at home, they are always abroad; for they think that the farther they go the more they will get, while you think that any movement may endanger what you have already. If they win a victory, they follow it up at once, and if they suffer a defeat, they scarcely fall back at all. As for their bodies, they regard them as expendable for their city's sake, as though they were not their own; but each man cultivates his own intelligence, again with a view to doing something notable for his city. If they aim at something and do not get it, they think that they have been deprived of what belonged to them already; whereas, if their enterprise is successful, they regard that success as nothing compared to what they will do next. Suppose they fail in some undertaking; they make good the loss immediately by setting their hopes in some other direction. Of them alone it may be said that they possess a thing almost as soon as they have begun to desire it, so quickly with them does action follow upon decision.

And so they go on working away in hardship and danger all the days of their lives, seldom enjoying their possessions because they are always adding to them. Their view of a holiday is to do what needs doing; they prefer hardship and activity to peace and quiet. In a word, they are by nature incapable of either living a quiet life themselves or of allowing anyone else to do so.

That is the character of the city which is opposed to you. Yet you still hang back; you will not see that the likeliest way of securing peace is this: only to use one's power in the cause of justice, but to make it perfectly plain that one is resolved not to tolerate aggression. On the contrary, your idea of proper behaviour is, firstly, to avoid harming others, and then to avoid being harmed yourselves, even if it is a matter of defending your own interests. Even if you had on your frontiers a power holding the same principles as you do, it is hard to see how such a policy could have been a success. But at the present time, as we have just pointed out to you, your whole way of life is out of date when compared with theirs. And it is just as true in politics as it is in any art or craft: new methods must drive out old ones. Athens, because of the very variety of her experience, is a far more modern state than you are.

The modern reputation of the Spartans is that of warriors who knew only how to fight. Actually they had made great pottery in the Archaic period (see page 112) and were famous for fine bronze objects. A few years ago a bronze caldron over five feet high was found in the grave of a princess of central Gaul about 500 B.C.; it had been carried overland from the Mediterranean. This stately chariot is a part of the frieze running about the neck of the vessel. Many scholars think it was made in Sparta (though others believe it originated in a Greek city in south Italy).

One of the Spartan kings, however, urged his fellow citizens not to rush into war with Athens, and put the Spartan nature in a different light than that suggested by the Corinthian ambassadors:

> As for being slow and cautious—which is the usual criticism made against us—there is nothing to be ashamed of in that. If you take something on before you are ready for it, hurry at the beginning will mean delay at the end. Besides, the city in which we live has always been

free and always famous. "Slow" and "cautious" can equally well be "wise" and "sensible." Certainly it is because we possess these qualities that we are the only people who do not become arrogant when we are successful, and who in times of stress are less likely to give in than others. We are not carried away by the pleasure of hearing ourselves praised when people are urging us towards dangers that seem to us unnecessary; and we are no more likely to give in shamefacedly to other people's views when they try to spur us on by their accusations.

Because of our well-ordered life we are both brave in war and wise in council. Brave, because self-control is based upon a sense of honour, and honour is based on courage. And we are wise because we are not so highly educated as to look down upon our laws and customs, and are too rigorously trained in self-control to be able to disobey them. We are trained to avoid being too clever in matter that are of no use—such as being able to produce an excellent theoretical criticism of one's enemies' dispositions, and then failing in practice to do quite so well against them. Instead we are taught that there is not a great deal of difference between the way we think and the way others think, and that it is impossible to calculate accurately events that are determined by chance.

The practical measures that we take are always based on the assumption that our enemies are not unintelligent. And it is right and proper for us to put our hopes in the reliability of our own precautions rather than in the possibility of our opponent making mistakes. There is no need to suppose that human beings differ very much one from another: but it is true that the ones who come out on top are the ones who have been trained in the hardest school.

Let us never give up this discipline which our fathers have handed down to us and which we still preserve and which has always done us good. Let us not be hurried, and in one short day's space come to a decision which will so profoundly affect the lives of men and their fortunes, the fates of cities and their national honour. We ought to take time over such a decision. And we, more than others, can afford to take time, because we are strong.

Years later an Athenian writer, Xenophon, prepared a little book, *Constitution of the Spartans,* in which he summed up a very widely held view of the Spartans:

> This state of Sparta, with good reason, outshines all other states in virtue; since she, and she alone, has made the attainment of a high standard of noble living a public duty.

7. The Qualities of Greek Civilization
(Pindar, *Pythian Ode* VIII, lines 95–97, translated by H. D. F. Kitto)

The following poetry does not bear directly on Athenian democracy
or imperialism, but it deserves the last word in a book on the ancient
Greeks. For Pindar's lines sum up briefly but magnificently the Greek
view of man's life:

A changeable creature, such is man; a shadow in a dream.
Yet when god-given splendor visits him
A bright radiance plays over him, and how sweet is life!

SOURCES OF QUOTATIONS

All quotations from Thucydides are in the translation by Rex Warner (Penguin Books, 1954); reprinted here by permission of the translator.

FURTHER READING

If you want further information on any subject in Greek history, the first place to look is in the major encyclopedias (*Americana, Britannica,* etc.). The best one-volume encyclopedia of ancient history is the <u>Oxford Classical Dictionary</u> (2d ed.; Oxford, 1970).

These works may refer you to books on the topic. Always check the first *copyright* date in a book (on the back of the title page); works on many aspects of Greek history more than 20 or 30 years old will be out of date on the facts they give.

Thousands of books have been written in many languages about the Greeks. I have selected a few which are recent, accurate, and generally interesting. The books which will be understood most easily are marked with an asterisk, but anyone interested in a special topic should try the others that deal with it. For paperback editions, only the series and number are given.

General Books: A good college textbook is G. W. Botsford and C. A. Robinson, Jr., *Hellenic History* (5th ed.; New York: Macmillan, 1969). A general study of ancient history is Chester G. Starr, *History of the Ancient World* (New York: Oxford University Press, 1965). <u>Will Durant</u>, <u>*Life of Greece**</u> (New York: Simon and Schuster, 1939), is a long, but clear, book; Robert Payne, *Ancient Greece** (New York: Norton, 1964), is briefer. Shorter yet are C. W. Bowra, *Classical Greece** (New York: Time, Inc., 1965); M. I. Finley, *The Ancient Greeks** (Viking C159); H. M. D. Kitto, *The Greeks* (Penguin A220).

On political ideas, see W. R. Agard, *What Democracy Meant to the Greeks** (Wisconsin 13), or Jill N. Claster, ed., *Athenian Democracy: Triumph or Travesty?* (New York: Holt, Rinehart and Winston, 1967). The best book on Sparta is H. Michell, *Sparta* (Cambridge 219).

The Greek method of fighting is sketched by F. E. Adcock, *Greek and Macedonian Art of War** (California 54); for battles, look in J. F. C. Fuller, *Military History of the Western World,* vol. I (New York: Funk & Wagnalls, 1954). Athletics are discussed by H. A. Harris, *Greek Athletes and Athletics** (Bloomington: Indiana University Press, 1966); see also John Kieran and Arthur Daley, *History of the Olympic Games** (Philadelphia: Lippincott, 1960).

The smell of the sea comes through in J. Holland Rose, *The Mediterranean in the Ancient World* (Cambridge: Cambridge University Press, 1933). Rhys Carpenter, *Beyond the Pillars of Heracles** (Delacorte Press, 1966), and Lionel Casson, *Ancient Mariners** (Minerva M17), will take you on distant voyages.

Early Greece: The Minoan and Mycenaean civilizations have attracted much attention. Good books are John Chadwick, *Decipherment of Linear B* (Random V172), a real detective story; Leonard Cottrell, *The Bull of Minos** (New York: Rinehart, 1958); M. I. Finley, *World of Odysseus** (Meridian M68); Frances Wilkins, *Ancient Crete** (New York: John Day, 1966). Joseph Alsop's *From the Silent Earth: A Report on the Greek Bronze Age* (New York: Harper & Row, 1964) is by a famous American newspaper writer.

Archeology in general is often described. See Kathleen M. Kenyon, *Beginning in Archaeology* (Praeger PPS 41); and on Greek excavations William A. MacDonald, *Progress into the Past* (New York: Macmillan, 1967). How about some scuba diving? George F. Bass, *Archaeology under Water** (New York: Praeger, 1966), and Peter Throckmorton, *The Lost Ships** (Boston: Little, Brown, 1964), are both exciting.

Greek Civilization: On daily life the best book is by Robert Flacelière, *Daily Life in Greece at the Time of Pericles* (New York: Macmillan, 1966); M. and C. H. B. Quennell's *Everyday Things in Ancient Greece** (2d ed.; New York: Putnam, 1954) is more often available. See also Charles Seltman, *Women in Antiquity* (New York: Collier, 1962); or R. E. Wycherley, *How the Greeks Built Cities* (2d ed.: London: Macmillan, 1962).

There are many books on Greek art. Inexpensive introductions are John Boardman, *Greek Art** (Praeger P172), and P. Devambez, *Greek Painting* (Viking CA1). Books illustrated with photographs by Max Hirmer are very good: *Greek Coins,* with C. M. Kraay (New York: Abrams, 1966);

Greek Temples, Theatres and Shrines, with H. Berve (1962); *Greek Sculpture,* with R. Lullies (1960); *Greek Vases,* with P. E. Arias (1962).

Major authors are briefly discussed by Edith Hamilton, *The Greek Way* (Norton N230); more fully by M. Hadas, *History of Greek Literature* (New York: Columbia University Press, 1950), and H. J. Rose, *Handbook of Greek Literature* (Dutton D66). Rex Warner, *Greeks and Trojans* (Michigan State College Press, 1953), retells the Trojan war; for mythology generally, see Edith Hamilton, *Mythology* (Boston: Little, Brown, 1942), or H. J. Rose, *Gods and Heroes of the Greeks* (Meridian M59).

Charles Seltman, *The Twelve Olympians* (New York: Crowell, 1960), gives a chapter to each of the major gods. Martin F. Nilsson, *Greek Folk Religion* (Harper TB78), relates Greek religion to daily life; W. K. C. Guthrie, *Greeks and Their Gods* (Beacon BP 2), is more general. Guthrie also has a straightforward book on *Greek Philosophers* (Harper TB 1008). Marshall Clagett, *Greek Science in Antiquity* (Collier BS 156), claims that anyone with high-school mathematics can understand his book; R. S. Brumbaugh, *Ancient Greek Gadgets and Machines* (New York: Crowell, 1966), takes up the earliest steam engine and other devices.

Biographies: John Gunther, *Alexander the Great* (New York: Random House, 1953); Geoffrey Household, *The Exploits of Xenophon* (New York: Random House, 1955); Harold Lamb, *Alexander of Macedon* (Garden City: Doubleday, 1946); Compton Mackenzie, *Pericles* (London: Hodder & Stoughton, 1937); Cora Mason, *Socrates: The Man Who Dared To Ask* (Boston: Beacon, 1953); Robert Payne, *The Gold of Troy* (New York: Funk & Wagnalls, 1958), on Heinrich Schliemann.

Stories: Winifred Bryher, *Gate to the Sea* (New York: Pantheon, 1958), on a Greek colony in Italy; L. Sprague de Camp, *An Elephant for Aristotle* (New York: Doubleday, 1958), on Alexander; James W. Ingles, *Test of Valor* (Philadelphia: Westminster, 1953), the conflict of an Athenian and Spartan at an Olympic race; Isabelle Lawrence, *Niko, Sorcerer's Apprentice* (New York: Viking, 1956), the building of the Parthenon; Naomi Mitchison, *Black Sparta* (London: Cape, 1933), not very favorable to Sparta; Alfred Powers, *Alexander's Horse* (New York: Longmans, 1959); Rex Warner, *Pericles the Athenian* (Boston: Little, Brown, 1963). Mary Renault has written a number of adult novels (*Last of the Wine, The King Must Die, Bull from the Sea, The Mask of Apollo*) which have been popular.

Many students of history find historical novels less exciting than the "real stuff," that is, the sources in which the Greeks themselves talk to us. Herodotus is one of the world's greatest storytellers; Thucydides' biting analysis is harder going, but worth the effort. Once ex-President Harry Truman was asked to name the ten best books; after the Bible he singled out Plutarch's *Lives:* "I've been quoting Plutarch all *my* life. You'd want some Plato, especially the parts about the old fellow who took poison." Above all there are Homer's *Iliad* and *Odyssey* and the Greek tragedies (I would suggest beginning with Sophocles' *Oedipus the King*).

The Penguin and Mentor paperback series have modern translations of these and other authors. Sappho's passionate love poetry is available in a translation by Willis Barnstone (Anchor A400).

All of us actually have already read a Greek source very carefully (or soon will)—a book on geometry. Look at a geometrical problem with its diagram and proof to see if you can detect in it the major qualities of Greek civilization: emphasis on the general rather than the specific; harmony and proportion; and logical analysis.

GLOSSARY

The following list provides brief identifications of major individuals and also definitions of unusual words in this book. As a guide to pronunciation I have marked, where necessary, the long vowels and the stressed syllables. For many important people in ancient history we do not know the date of birth or even sometimes of death; but as far as possible chronological indications are suggested.

Academy, 4th-century research institute in philosophy founded by Plato just outside Athens

Achaeans (a-kē′-ans), a name given by Homer to the Greeks who fought at Troy

Achilles (a-kil′-ēz), main hero in Homer's *Iliad*

Acragas (ak′-ra-gaz), state on south coast of Sicily, called Agrigentum in Roman times

Acropolis (a-krop′ō-lis), fortified hill in Athens on which the Parthenon was erected

Aegean Sea (ē-jē′-an), branch of Mediterranean Sea on which Greek culture was centered

Aegospotami (ē-gos-pot′-a-mī), site on Hellespont where the Athenians lost a final naval battle in 405

Aeschylus (es′-ki-lus), 525–456, Athenian author of many tragedies, including *Agamemnon* and *Persians*

Aesop (ē-sop), legendary author of animal fables

Agamemnon (ag-a-mem′-non), tragedy by Aeschylus about the murder of the king of Mycenae who commanded the Greeks at Troy

Agora (ag′-ō-ra), assembly place for citizens of a Greek *polis*, as at Athens

Alexander, 356–23, king of Macedonia who conquered Persian empire

Anaxagoras (an-ak-sag′-ō-ras), about 500–428, philosopher and scientist

Antigone (an-tig′-ō-ne), tragedy by Sophocles about the daughter of Oedipus

Antipater (an-tip′-a-ter), died 319, general of Alexander

Aphrodite (af-rō-dī'-tē), goddess of love

Apollo (a-pol'-ō), god of wisdom and music, worshipped especially at Delphi and Delos

Arbela (ar-bē'-la), site in northern Mesopotamia where Alexander defeated Darius in 331

Arcadia (ar-kā'-di-a), mountainous region in central Peloponnesus

Archaic art, style of Greek art from about 700 to 500

Archimedes (ar-ki-mē'-dēz), died 212, mathematician at Syracuse

archon eponymos (ar'-kon ep-on'-i-mus), official elected yearly at Athens who gave his name to the year (493, for example, was the "archonship of Themistocles")

Areopagus (ar-ē-op'-a-gus), hill west of Acropolis at Athens, seat of an ancient council

Ares (ā'-rēz), god of war

Argos (ar'-gos), major state in northeast Peloponnesus which often opposed Sparta

Aristarchus (ar-is-tar'-kus), about 310–230, astronomer who guessed that the earth went around the sun

aristocracy, a dominant social group distinguished by birth rather than solely by wealth

Aristogeiton (ar-is-tō-jī'-ton), one of the slayers of Hipparchus in 514, celebrated by the Athenians as a tyrannicide

Aristophanes (ar-is-tof'-a-nēz), about 450–385, major writer of comedies at Athens

Aristotle (ar'-is-tot-l), 384–322, philosopher and scientist, teacher of Alexander

Artemis (ar'-te-mis), goddess of hunting and wild animals

Artemisium, Cape (ar-te-mish'-i-um), northern point of Euboea where the Greeks fought the Persians by sea in 480

Asclepius (as-klē'-pi-us), god of healing, especially worshipped at Epidaurus

Athena (a-thē'-na), goddess of wisdom and arts, patroness of Athens

Athens, state in east-central Greece, dominant in Aegean in 5th century

Bacchae (bak'-ē), tragedy by Euripides about followers of Dionysus

black-figure pottery, style of pottery made at Athens in 6th century in which figures are black on red background

Boeotia (bē-ō'-shi-a), geographical district north of Athens, containing Thebes and other states

Byzantium (bi-zan'-shi-um), state at entrance to Black Sea, the modern Istanbul

Cambyses (kam-bī'-sēz), king of Persian empire, 530–522

cella (sel'-a), central room of temple which contained statue of god

Chaeronea (ker-ō-nē'-a), state in Boeotia, site of defeat of Greeks by Philip in 338

Chalcis (kal'sis), state in Euboea which led in colonizing movement

Chios (kī'os), island off Asia Minor coast

chiton (kī'-tōn), garment hanging from shoulders

choregus (kō-rē'-gus), producer of play at Athens

Cimon (sī'-mon), about 512–450, Athenian admiral who expanded Delian league

Cleomenes (klē-om'-e-nēz), king of Sparta about 520 to 490, who consolidated Spartan power

Cleon (klē'on), average Athenian citizen in this book (there actually was a democratic politician by the name of Cleon, killed in battle in 422)

Cleopatra (klē-ō-pā'-tra), 69–30, last Ptolemaic ruler of Egypt

Clisthenes (klīs'-the-nēz), Athenian leader who established democracy in 508

Cnossus (nos'-us), Minoan palace on north coast of Crete

colony, Greek state founded abroad which was independent of its mother state

Corinth, state at isthmus of Corinth which was a main trading center

Crete (krēt), island on south side of Aegean Sea

Croesus (krē'-sus), king of Lydia overthrown by Persians in 547

Cyclades (sik'-la-dēz), islands in center of Aegean Sea

Cyrus (sī'rus), king who founded Persian empire, 550 to 530

Darius (da-rī'-us), king of Persian empire, 521–486, who organized its satrapies

Dark Ages, period between 1100 and 700 during which writing was not used

Delian league, association formed in 478 to fight the Persians, the root of the Athenian empire

Delos (dē'los), island sacred to Apollo in the Cyclades group of islands

Delphi (del'-fī), shrine of Apollo famous for its oracle

Deme (dēm), unit of local government in Athens

Demeter (dē-mē'-ter), goddess of agriculture, worshipped especially at Eleusis

Democritus (dē-mok'-ri-tus), about 460–370, philosopher who advanced atomic theory

Demosthenes (dē-mos'-the-nēz), 384–322, orator and statesman at Athens who opposed Philip of Macedonia

Diogenes (dī-oj'-e-nēz), about 400–325, Cynic philosopher

Dionysius I (dī-ō-nish'-i-us), tyrant of Syracuse from 405 to 367

Dionysus (dī-ō-nī'-sus), god who gave emotional release to men through wine and revels

Dipylon gate (dip'-i-lon), gate on west side of Athens outside which extended a great cemetery

drachma (drak'ma), basic silver coin weighing at Athens a little over 4 grams

Eleusis (ē-lū'-sis), sanctuary of Demeter 12 miles from Athens

Empedocles (em-ped'-ō-klēz), about 493–433, philosopher who proposed that earth, air, fire, and water were the basic elements

ephor (ef'-or), one of group of five officials elected annually at Sparta

Epicurus (ep-i-kū'-rus), 342–271, founder of Epicurean philosophy

Epidaurus (ep-i-dō'-rus), state in northeastern Peloponnesus, site of a major sanctuary of Asclepius

Erasistratus (er-a-sis'-tra-tus), doctor at Alexandria about 300 who studied the blood system

Erechtheum (er-ek-thē'-um), temple built in late 5th century on Acropolis

Eretria (e-re′-tri-a), state in Euboea which fought with Chalcis

Euboea (ū-bē′-a), island lying off coast of Athens and Boeotia

Euclid (ū′klid), author about 300 of *Elements,* a survey of geometry

Euripides (ū-rip′-i-dēz), 485–406, Athenian author of many tragedies including *Medea* and *Bacchae*

Eurotas river (ū-rō′-tas), small stream watering the Spartan plain

Evans, Sir Arthur, 1851–1941, English archeologist who excavated Cnossus

fresco, painting on plaster wall

games, festival in ancient Greece, usually involving athletic contests

Gela (jā′-la), state in southeastern Sicily

Gelon (jē′lon), tyrant of Syracuse who repelled Carthaginian invasion in 480

Geometric pottery, style of pottery about 900–700 which was usually decorated with abstract symbols

Gorgias (gor′-ji-as), about 483–376, founder of study of rhetoric at Athens

Granicus river (gra-nī′-kus), site of first battle in Alexander's invasion of Persian empire in 334

Harmodius (har-mō′-di-us), one of the slayers of Hipparchus in 514, celebrated by Athenians as a tyrannicide

Hector (hek′-ter), chief warrior of Trojans in *Iliad,* killed by Achilles

Helicon, Mount (hel′-i-kon), mountain in Boeotia, the muses of which taught Hesiod to be a poet

Hellespont (hel′-es-pont), strait leading from Aegean to Black Sea, now called the Dardanelles

helot (hel′-ot), peasant in Sparta who was required to furnish food to the Spartan warriors

Hephaestus (hē-fes′-tus), god of metalworking

Hera (hē′-ra), goddess wife of Zeus, patroness of women and marriage

Heracles (her′-a-klēz), hero who carried out twelve great "labors" for men and was admitted to Mount Olympus

Heraclitus (her-a-klī′-tus), philosopher shortly after 500 who asserted that everything constantly changed

Hermes (hur′mēz), god who protected wayfarers and commerce; also messenger of gods

Hermus river (her′-mus), river in western Asia Minor, now called Gediz

hero, a great man at whose grave sacrifices were carried out on behalf of a local community

Herodotus (hē-rod′-ō-tus), about 484 to after 430, historian of Persian wars; the "Father of History" as the first great historical writer

Herophilus (her-ō′-fi-lus), doctor at Alexandria about 300 who traced the nervous system

Hesiod (Hē′-sē-od), poet about 700 who wrote *Works and Days*

Hestia (hes′ti-a), goddess of the hearth

hexameter, a poetic line consisting of six feet; used in epic poetry especially *himation*-(hi-mat'-i-on), shawl consisting of rectangle of wool which could be draped around the shoulders

Hipparchus (hi-par'-kus), tyrant of Athens murdered in 514; also the greatest astronomer of the Hellenistic era, about 190–126

Hippias (hip'-i-as), brother of Hipparchus and tyrant of Athens to 510

Hippocrates (hi-pok'-ra-tēz), 469–399, first major writer on Greek medicine

Hippodamus (hip-pō-dā'-mus), 5th-century city-planner who laid out the Piraeus in a regular plan

Homer, a name attached to *Iliad* and *Odyssey*, the first great works in Greek literature which probably assumed their final form in 8th century

hoplite (hop'-līt), heavily armored infantry warrior, organized in a phalanx

hybris (hū'-bris), human pride which goes beyond the bounds which the gods will allow

Hydaspes river (hī-das'-pēz), site of Alexander's battle against Porus in 327, now the Jhelum river

Hyphasis river (hī-fa'-sis), tributary of Indus river at which Alexander ended his advance

Ictinus (ik-tī'-nus), major architect of the Parthenon

Iliad (il'-i-ad), epic poem ascribed to Homer, dealing with the anger of Achilles and its results during the Trojan war

Ionia (ī-ō'-ni-a), region on west coast of Asia Minor inhabited by Greeks who spoke the Ionian dialect

Isocrates (ī-sok'-ra-tēz), 436–338, teacher of rhetoric at Athens

isonomia (ī-sō-nō-mi'-a), equal rights under law, a term used by Clisthenes at Athens

Issus (is'-us), site of battle by Alexander against Darius in 333, in northern Syria

Jocasta (jō-kas'-ta), wife of Oedipus, king of Thebes

kore (kō'-rē), standing female statue in archaic art

kouros (koo'-ros), standing male statue in archaic art

Laurium (lav'-ri-on), site of Athenian silver mines

Leonidas (lē-on'-i-das), king of Sparta who fell at Thermopylae in 480

Lesbos (lez'-bos), island off west coast of Asia Minor, home of Sappho

Leuctra (lūk'tra), site in Boeotia where Thebes smashed Spartan power in 371

Linear B, a syllabic form of writing used in Mycenaean Greece

Lyceum (lī-sē'-um), teaching and research institute in philosophy and science founded by Aristotle just outside Athens

Lycurgus (li-kur'-gus), legendary Spartan lawgiver

Lydia (lid'-i-a), kingdom in west-central Asia Minor

Lysander (lī-san'-der), Spartan leader who defeated Athens in 404

Macedonia (mas-e-dō'-nī-a), kingdom north of ancient Greece

Maeander river (mē-an'-der), river in western Asia Minor, now called Büyük Menderes

Marathon, site in Athens where Athenians defeated the Persians in 490

Mardonius (mar-dō'-ni-us), Persian commander at battle of Plataea in 479

megaron (meg'-a-ron), rectangular room with foreporch serving as kernel of Mycenaean palace and as root of the temple plan

Menander (me-nan'-der), 342–291, author of comedies at Athens

Menelaus (men-e-lā'-us), king of Sparta, husband of Helen, in *Iliad*

Messenia (me-sē'-ni-a), district in Peloponnesus west of Sparta, the helots of which had to provide food to the Spartans

metope (met'-ō-pē), square slab between triglyphs on temple, often sculptured

Miletus (mī-lē'-tus), a major state in Ionia

Minoan civilization, culture centered in Crete in 2d millennium B.C.

mosaic, decoration (usually on floors) composed of pebbles or small square stones

muses, spirits who encouraged poets; eventually the Greeks recognized nine muses

Mycale (mik'-a-lē), site of naval defeat of Persians in 479

Mycenae (mī-sē'-nē), palace and fortress in northeast Peloponnesus

Nike (nī'-kē), goddess of victory

obol (ob'-ol), small silver coin, 1/6 of a drachma

Odyssey (od'-i-si), epic poem assigned to Homer dealing with the wanderings of Odysseus for ten years after the fall of Troy

Oedipus the King (ē-di-pus), tragedy by Sophocles about a king of Thebes who married his mother (hence the Oedipus complex in modern psychology)

oligarchy, a system of government by a few citizens (usually the wealthy ones)

Olympia, religious center in western Peloponnesus where Olympic games were held

Olympias (ō-limp'-i-as), mother of Alexander of Macedonia

Olympus, Mount (ō-lim'-pus), mountain in Thessaly (9571 feet); legendary home of gods

oracle, religious prophecy usually in veiled language; also the center giving such prophecies, as the temple of Apollo at Delphi

Orientalizing pottery, the style following Geometric pottery; human figures and freehand drawing are prominent in this style

Orphics (or'-fiks), a religious group holding mystical beliefs which they believed had been handed down from Orpheus

ostracism, a constitutional device at Athens by which unpopular leaders could be sent into exile for ten years

Paestum (pes'tum), Greek state near Naples which has some of the best preserved temples

papyrus, paper made from a reed which grows in Egypt

Parmenio (par-men'-i-ō), a chief general of Alexander

Parthenon (par'-the-non), temple to Athena on the Acropolis, built 447–438

Patroclus (pa-trō'-klus), friend of Achilles, killed by Hector in the *Iliad*

pediment, the triangular gable at each end of a temple, often decorated with statues depicting a mythical event

Peloponnesian war, 431–404, fought between Athens and Sparta and resulting in complete defeat of Athens

Peloponnesus (pel-ō-po-nē'-sos), southern part of Greece; literally the word means "island of Pelops," after a mythical figure

peltast (pel'-tast), lightly armored infantry soldier

peplos (pep'-los), garment of long rectangular cloth, draped and pinned at the shoulders

Pergamum (pur'ga-mum), state in northwest Asia Minor prominent in Hellenistic period

Pericles (per'-i-klēz), about 495 to 429, Athenian leader during its period of empire

Perioikoi (per-i-oi'-koi), citizens of Sparta without a vote

Persepolis (per-sep'-ō-lis), treasury fortress in southern Persia

phalanx (fā'-langks), body of infantry hoplites

Phalaris (fal'-a-ris), 6th-century tyrant of Acragas famous for his cruelty

pharos (far'-os), lighthouse, the most famous of which was at Alexandria

Phidias (fid'-i-as), 5th-century Athenian sculptor, whose major works were on the Acropolis and at Olympia

Phidippides (fī-dip'-pi-dēz), long-distance runner at time of Marathon

Philip, king of Macedonia, 359–336, father of Alexander

Pindar (pin'-dar), about 518 to 438, great poet of odes in honor of athletic victors and on other occasions

Piraeus (pī-rē'-us), port of Athens

Pisistratus (pi-sis'-tra-tus), tyrant of Athens, 541–527

Plataea (pla-tē'-a), site of Persian defeat in Boeotia in 479

Plato (plā'-tō), 428–348, pupil of Socrates, a major philosopher

Pnyx (niks), hill west of Acropolis on which Athenian Assembly met

polis (pō'-lis), Greek term for independent state which had a single political center

Polyclitus (pol-i-klī'-tus), 5th-century sculptor

Polygnotus (pol-ig-nō'-tus), 5th-century painter

Porus (pō'-rus), Indian king who opposed Alexander at Hydaspes river in 337

Poseidon (pō-sī'-don), god of sea and earthquakes

Praxiteles (praks-it'-e-lēz), 4th-century sculptor of *Hermes* and other works

Priam (prī'-am), king of Troy in *Iliad*

Propylaea (prop-i-lē'-a), entryway to Acropolis

Protogeometric pottery, style of pottery with simple designs from about 1050 to 900

Ptolemy (tol'-e-mi), founder of Hellenistic dynasty in Egypt in late 4th century

Pylos (pī'-los), palace of Mycenaean period in western Peloponnesus

Pythagoras (pi-thag'-ō-ras), 6th-century philosopher who believed in transmigration

red-figure pottery, style of pottery made at Athens about 525 to 400 in which figures are red on black background

Rhodes (rōdz), island off southwestern corner of Asia Minor
Roxane (rok-san′-e), wife of Alexander of Macedonia

Salamis (sal′-a-mis), island off Athens, site of naval battle against Persians in 480
Samos (sā′-mos), island off west coast of Asia Minor, home of Pythagoras
Sappho (saf′-ō), poetess active about 600 on island of Lesbos
Saronic gulf (sa-ron′-ik), gulf south of Athens, part of Aegean Sea
satrapy (sā′-tra-pi), province of Persian empire
Schliemann, Heinrich, 1822–1890, archeologist who excavated Troy and Mycenae
Segesta (se-jes′-ta), state in north Sicily
Seleucus (sē-lū′-kus), general of Alexander who founded Seleucid dynasty in Syria and Mesopotamia
Socrates (sok′-ra-tēz), 469–399, philosophic critic at Athens
Solon (sō′-lon), archon at Athens in 594, when he reformed government and laws
sophist (sof′-ist), teacher at Athens in late 5th century, emphasizing rhetoric and skillful argument
Sophocles (sof′-ō-klēz), 496–406, Athenian author of many tragedies including *Antigone* and *Oedipus the King*
sophrosyne (sof-ro′-si-nē), wisdom which recognizes the limitations of mankind
Sparta, state in south-central Peloponnesus famous for its way of life
stoa (stō′-a), colonnade open on one side to the Agora, often with shops at the back
Stoicism (stō′-i-sizm), Hellenistic philosophy founded by Zeno, who talked in the *stoa* at Athens
Sybaris (sib′-a-ris), state in south Italy destroyed in 510
Syracuse, important state on east coast of Sicily

Thales (thā′-lēz), first philosopher, shortly after 600
Thebes (thēbz), principal state in Boeotia
Themistocles (thē-mis′-tō-klēz), about 528 to 462, Athenian statesman who helped lead the Greeks against the Persian invasion of 480
Thermopylae (ther-mop′-i-lē), pass between mountains and sea held by Leonidas against Persian invasion in 480
Theseus (thē′-sūs), mythical hero at Athens who killed the Minotaur
Thessaly (thes′-a-lī), district in northern Greece
tholos (thō′-los), round building used as tomb at Mycenae or council chamber at Athens
Thucydides (thū-sid′-i-dēz), about 460 to 400, Athenian historian of the Peloponesian war
Thurii (thoo′-ri-i), state founded in south Italy in 443
Tiryns (ti′-rinz), palace in Mycenaean period near Mycenae
trireme (trī′-rēm), galley in which rowers sat in groups of three
Troy, fortress attacked by Achaeans in *Iliad*
Tyre (tīr), a principal Phoenician state

Ventris, Michael, 1922–1956, British architect who deciphered Linear B

Xenophanes (zē-nof'-a-nēz), 6th-century philosopher
Xenophon (zen'-ō-fon), 4th-century historian
Xerxes (zurk'-sēz), king of Persian empire, 485–465

Zeno (zē'-nō), 335–263, founder of Stoic philosophy
Zeus (zūs), god of the sky, chief of Olympian gods